T0162804

Qualities of Sound Christian Education

Biblical Advice for Christian Schools, Parents, & Homeschools

Kevin F. Brownlee

WestBow Press books may be ordered through booksellers or by contacting:

WestBow Press
A Division of Thomas Nelson & Zondervan
1663 Liberty Drive
Bloomington, IN 47403
www.westbowpress.com
1 (866) 928-1240

ISBN: 978-1-4908-2442-0 (sc)
ISBN: 978-1-4908-2441-3 (hc)
ISBN: 978-1-4908-2444-4 (e)

Library of Congress Control Number: 2014901840

Printed in the United States of America.

WestBow Press rev. date: 3/18/2014

Contents

Acknowledgements

I wish to thank these people who directly helped with this book:

My Wife Bunny Brownlee
My Daughter Kallee Brownlee
Matt Henry
Preston Sprinkle
Bryan Hughes

Prologue

In a society where the term *Christian* seems to be losing some of its original meaning, and likewise, where some "Christian" schools seem to be succumbing to pressures to be more like secular public schools, or compromising biblical principles to attract students or financial support or even to avoid ridicule, it is good to know, review, evaluate, and apply what qualities make up sound Christian education. *Sound* is a term taken from Titus 2:1 where Paul said to teach with *sound* teachings. God blesses those who are obedient to His Word, the Bible, and that applies to educational endeavors and institutions as well as individual Christian lives.

In the education system today, there is a battle for the world view of the minds and hearts of our children. That battle has been won by the Enemy in the public schools, but do you know he has mustered up forces and is concentrating efforts to attack *Christian* schools and home schooling? The battle and attackers are real, as mentioned in Ephesians 6:12, even in the seemingly safe haven of Christian education, and at stake is the future effectiveness of our children for God.

If you are a Christian parent, teacher, or Christian school staff member, are you able to recognize these attacks? Do you know how to fight and win the battles? Do you know the required qualities for Christian education to effectively withstand attacks, and win ensuing battles? Do you know the required qualities of Christian education to give students strength, power, self-discipline, and a sound mind in their lives of serving and glorifying God? These qualities need to be established by biblical principles. They can also be used as a litmus test to evaluate Christian schools, and then used to strengthen that school for effectiveness in the lives of students.

The goal of this book is to outline sound biblical qualities of effective Christian education, and to outfit the educator with the tools required to be effective, and to withstand the attacks of enemies of biblically based education. If followed, the educator will ensure that his or her students will fulfill God's purpose in their lives. God will complete the good work He started in their lives (Philippians 1:6), and the student will not depart from the foundation of sound biblical teaching (Proverbs 22:6). Sound Christian education done correctly ensures both.

Every one of us has asked "What is my purpose in life? Why am I here?" I believe God answers those questions in three passages in Scripture:

- "Everyone who is called by My name, Whom I have created for My glory; I have formed him, yes, I have made him." (Isaiah 43:7). We are created for the purpose of glorifying God.
- "Therefore, whether you eat or drink, or whatever you do, do all to the glory of God." (1 Corinthians 10:31). We are to glorify God in everything we do.
- "And we know that all things work together for good to those who love God, to those who are the called according to His purpose. For whom He foreknew, He also predestined to be conformed to the image of His Son," (Romans 8:28-29). We are to love God, do His purpose for us, which is primarily to become like Jesus.

This book will help educators and parents lay the groundwork for ensuring God's purpose is fulfilled in their student or child.

Introduction

Christians are told in Scripture to shine as lights in the world: "…that you may become blameless and harmless, children of God without fault in the midst of a crooked and perverse generation, among whom you shine as lights in the world" (Philippians 2:15). And Jesus said "You are light in the world…" (Matthew 5:14-16). This metaphor insinuates that Christians should endeavor to be equated with godliness, which is like light shining in darkness. Conversely, worldliness is generally considered ungodliness and is equated with darkness. (1 John 2:15; Ephesians 6:12). Our world is filled with ungodly darkness, and Christian schools should thus shine brightly when compared to worldly schooling.

But, what does that mean? How do Christian schools shine? What are the differences between Christian and public schooling? Can there be Christian education that is worldly? What qualities make up that "light in the world" the Bible talks about? In which areas should Christian schooling be obedient to God, and what is it that He requires? What basis or standard should Christian schools use for their purpose or for evaluating their effectiveness? This book will answer those questions, give examples, and provide advice and instruction on all of these issues.

This book will glean heavily from God's Word, the Bible, to derive the qualities of sound Christian schooling and education. Not only listing these qualities, but explaining *why* they are important and required of a Christian school, as well as how to attain and teach these qualities. Biblical Christianity uses teaching, and the mind: We are to read the Bible, ponder it, and intellectually apply what we read to our life. To a Christian, this is not optional but *required* and becomes the reasons for and successes of Christian schools.

Education is rapidly changing. We all have seen the changes in the public/government schools in America within most of our lifetimes. Even the definition of "education" has changed, and it parallels the changes in our schools:

> **Modern definition from Webster's Dictionary:**
> "Education is the act or process of imparting or acquiring general knowledge and of developing the powers of reasoning and judgment. The act or process of imparting or acquiring particular knowledge or skills, as for a profession."[1]
>
> **Original definition from Webster's Dictionary (origins from about 1535):**
> "Education is the bringing up, as a child; instruction; formation of manners. Education comprehends all that series of instruction and discipline, which is intended to enlighten the understanding, correct the temper, and form the manners and habits of youth, and fit them for usefulness in their future stations. To give children a good education in manners, arts, and science, is important; to give them a religious education is indispensable; and an immense responsibility rests on parents and guardians who neglect these duties."[2]

Notice the deletion of that last sentence, and I am sure you have also noticed the results of that last sentence being removed from our education process. Or was that sentence removed because it is no longer true of the majority of our education? Whichever came first, the change in the definition or the change in education, the reality is a diminished effort of teaching manners and habits and certainly the removal of religious education from the majority of schools. Praise God for Christian schools, and Christian home schooling! There you will find (hopefully) a complete understanding of the indispensable link between biblical religion and education as the older definition states. That link between God's Word and education is not only "an immense responsibility" of parents and guardians, but also a *requirement.* Sound Christian schooling takes that requirement and the responsibility of administering it seriously. I am reminded of a quote from Martin Luther that should become a mantra for sound Christian schooling:

> "I am much afraid that schools will prove to be the gates of hell unless they diligently labor in explaining the Holy Scriptures, engraving them in the hearts of youth. **I advise no one to place their child where the Scriptures do not reign paramount. Every institution in which men are not increasingly occupied with the word of God must become corrupt**."[3] (emphasis added)

Training up a child in the biblical nurture and admonition (discipline) of the Lord (Proverbs 22:6 and Ephesians 6:4) is a *huge* responsibility that every Christian parent should take very seriously and obey. I realize there is good debate among evangelical Christians as to how children should be educated, and I do not wish to cast stones at any true Christian parent's decision. I do not wish to cause division among believers, *but to sow unity.* In Romans 14, Paul writes how we are to maintain unity among believers, even if we hold differing views on issues (such as education) that are not core doctrinal issues. I just ask that we respect those parents' decisions with love, and look to your own understanding of what God is requiring of you, and obey that. By reading this book, you most likely fall into the camp of agreeing with Christian schooling or Christian home schooling. If not, I encourage you to not put this book down but to read it through so as to not quell the opportunity for God to speak to you (I am not claiming to be God, only a conveyor of what I have learned), to understand the Christian schooling point of view, or to relate your opposing views without misunderstandings.

Christian schoolers should refrain from condemning the public schools, but should instead solidify in their mind why they choose Christian schooling over public schooling so that when asked they can provide a patient, loving, clearly understandable description of their decision. Christians are to be humble (but not weak or shy) loving witnesses for Christ as lights in the world, not arrogant or self-righteous who condemn others for decisions that may differ from theirs.

The Bible was written over a span of about 1,500 years. When reviewing the Bible for references to education of children, I came to the conclusion that the only times godly families sent their children to government schools was when they were forced to while in bondage. All other times it seems that they home schooled or schooled together with other godly families (although specific references to that are vague, we can assume so with relative validity), and at their church or synagogue. Holman's Bible Dictionary covers education in biblical times very well, and I encourage you to look it up.[4] We do know for sure that God placed education of children squarely on the shoulders of parents, and that education must include the oracles of God such as His Truths and doctrines, and include them in all aspects throughout the day. In other words, biblically based education. Deuteronomy 6:6-7 says "And these words which I command you today shall be in your heart. You shall teach them diligently to your children, and shall talk of them when you sit in your house, when you walk by the way, when you lie down, and when you rise up."

All parents are home schoolers, and all Christian homes are Christian schools to some extent. Kids are like sponges, and will absorb what occurs in the home. Most Christian schools recognize this and state they go along side of the Christian parent in training and educating the child. Some parents cannot or cannot adequately teach their children in the home, so must pursue education outside the home. Hopefully, Christian parents will pursue biblically based education to fulfill this and to, as Hebrews 13:21 says, "Equip you with everything good for doing His will."

Only recently in our country's history has the major form of schooling and the resultant education not been based in the bible. I assume you would agree that public schools are the major venue of education today, and although it may include some biblical references and employ some Christian teachers or administrators, public schooling today is no longer biblically based, and certainly not considered "Christian education".

Today, Christian parents fall into one of these three categories:

The first group are those Christian parents that neglect or dismiss the requirement of biblical based education all together, or at best, relegate bible based education to a few family bible devotions and/or Sunday school assuming that will suffice as well for "Monday school, Tuesday school, etc." I have many dear Christian friends and relatives whose decisions fit here, and still applaud some of their efforts. If you are a parent in this category, I encourage you to please read this book anyway.

The second group of Christian parents are those that look into their options of biblically based Christian schooling or home schooling, and find that the choices are either burdensome, or prohibitively expensive. (I would argue both of which could be construed as either selfishness, or lack of trust in God that He will enable them and provide for them to obey His requirement. However, I am not oblivious to the few situations where public schooling *is* the only option). So they do one of two things: Opt for public education anyway and resolve to make the best of it as God would lead (Home devotions, church youth group, or other Christian teaching). Or, they give up (or give in) and choose public education and let it go at that. Most of those parents will then come up with reasons, excuses, or rationalizations to justify their choice. Some may consciously or unconsciously rely on the mercy and sovereignty of God to care for and use their child for His glory. If you are a parent in this category, I hope you will continue to read this book because I believe you will find plenty of help that will benefit you and your children that God loves so dearly.

The third group of parents is those who choose to home school their children, or send them to a Christian school. I know that most of them sacrifice to do so. If you are a parent in this category, or an educator that a parent has entrusted their children's education with, then this book is for both of you.

This book will cover a lot of biblical guidelines for training and educating children either at home or at a Christian school. It can also serve the Christian parent as a resource of what to look for when searching for a sound Christian school to educate their children, as well as for anyone involved in Christian schooling. However, this book's primary purpose is not to present the *reason* for choosing Christian education, although it should indirectly give those reasons. There are many excellent organizations, books, blogs, or web sites devoted to the reasons a parent should choose Bible based Christian education. One that comes to my mind (because it was the first one that grabbed my attention as I pursued obedience in this area), is "WARNING! PUBLIC SCHOOLS AREN'T FOR CHRISTIANS! A Biblical Perspective by Richard "Little Bear" Wheeler".[5] Another great resource is DiscoverChristianSchools.com. There, you will find biblical information on such topics as "What the Bible says about education", "Why money is never an issue", and "10 reasons to send your child to a Christian school", as well as resources and links to a plethora of useful information for parents and educators.

I mentioned earlier that parents in Bible times only had their children educated by the government when they were in *bondage*. Think about that. Are today's parents of public/government school children in bondage? Could it be they are in bondage to a lifestyle so they think they cannot afford Christian education? Are they in bondage to low self-esteem or lack of trust in God that they could not possibly home school their kids? Bondage comes in different forms such as idolatry (an idol is something we value more than God and His will), compromise, laziness, or self-centeredness. Something to think about isn't it?

It takes a mature Christian parent to understand the big picture of parenting/training/educating their child: God has a purpose for their child, and if the child is, or will become a Christian, it involves spiritual growth, serving Jesus, and ministry to others. Philippians 3:12-14 is about this purpose and goal, and a portion of the passage says: "...I press on, that I may lay hold of that for which Christ Jesus has also laid hold of me..." Christian schooling exists to facilitate or go along side a Christian parent's training of their child for God's purposes so their child may "lay hold" of that purpose. Remember, if God requires you to do something, He will give you the means or tools to obey Him and do it, including the funds or resources for your child's attendance in a Christian school, or Christian based home schooling.

In his book "Millstones & Stumbling Blocks", Bradley Heath makes a very good statement concerning Christian parents' understanding their responsibilities to provide a thoroughly Christian education, and to stick with it: "Within the boundaries of God's providence, parents must take direct responsibility for their children's education and ensure that it is thoroughly Christian. All educational decisions should be based on principled obedience to the Word of God. It is not enough to recognize and reject the bad fruit of public schooling. We must be proactive, not reactive, or we will do the right things for the wrong reasons. Reactionary decisions lack the staying power and conviction necessary to sacrificially provide our children a thoroughly Christian education. Reactionary parents often return to public school when they find Christian education too hard, inconvenient, or expensive."[6]

In addition to Heath's statements for parents' choosing Christian education, and to not give up on it, he brings up an additional point; one that Jesus was making in the Gospel of John chapter 15 that true

Christians will bear fruit. Parents are to provide the best opportunity for children to bear the fruit He was talking about. Christian education *is* that opportunity, and Christian schools or Christian home schools are responsible to provide such an environment and such a "growth of the branch" that permits the student to bring forth that fruit.

The purposes and basic Christian fundamentals of Christian home schools and Christian schools are pretty much the same, however there are some obvious differences between the two such as the location of the classroom facility, set schedule, student interaction, administration, etc. Those differences make writing this book difficult because some of the topics of one may not apply to the other, so I decided it is best to choose one to address the focus of this book to, and ask the other to "bear with me". The majority of the qualities of sound Christian education are the same for both, but Christian schools have more issues that need addressing so I chose to write this book from a Christian school point of view to Christian schools. Thank you for your understanding.

Although written from a Christian schooling point of view and to Christian schools, the elements in this book will also help:

- Home school parents to have a biblical perspective of the qualities of their home schooling curriculum and purpose. Advise the training of children for lives of serving and glorifying God in whatever they do.
- Christian colleges and universities to have a biblical perspective and focus, as well as to evaluate the purpose and focus using a biblical standard of evaluation. The principles of sound Christian education are not specific to grades K-12, but to all educational institutions and endeavors.
- Parents to develop a biblically well-grounded view of Christian schooling.

- Parents to have biblically well-grounded qualities or elements as a basis for choosing a Christian school for their children. (And, to hold their chosen Christian school accountable to these elements).
- Leaders and staff of Christian schools to evaluate their school and to remedy any deficiencies found. To also evaluate the spiritual effectiveness of their schooling.
- Trustees or possible future trustees of Christian schools to understand and/or implement what qualities and biblical doctrine make up a sound Christian school. To know God's criteria when hiring an Administrator or Teachers. To recognize attacks from the enemies of the school. To offer advice and suggestions on fundraising.
- Every Christian to evaluate their heart for obedience to God and God's Word in the area of training and schooling children and the requirements of doing so, as well as realizing the threats, attacks, and obstacles associated with that obedience.

While reading this book, keep a lookout for what I call the "elements of a sound Christian school". They are short statements or key points at the culmination of that related topic. They will then be compiled in the last chapter as a form of summary. But don't cheat and go to the back of the book to find them without first reading the book, you wouldn't allow that in your school now would you?! When you do get through this book, I would suggest using those elements as daily or weekly reminders of quality Christian educations. Maybe take each of those statements and put them on a sticky note or pop up reminder on your computer to keep you and your school focused on these key points.

I believe God places a love for something in our heart that some call a burden, others call a strong will or desire, to learn all we can, and then pass that on to others. God does so to use us as tools to further His purposes of some sort or another. It usually enriches us as well as others. It is my hope and prayer that my love for Christian education, coupled with my love for God and God's Word is brought together in this book, and portrayed to you in a loving manner as an effort to ensure Christian education is truly CHRIST-ian.

Chapter 1

The Standard

Editor's note: Although this book is valuable to a wide audience such as Christian school administrators, teachers, home schoolers, Christian colleges, parents, authors of Christian school textbooks, and church leaders, it is impossible to address the general diction to everyone, so it is primarily written as if the reader is a leader in a Christian grade school.

Christian schooling: what an awesome opportunity and safer haven for Christian parents who are disgusted with what is being taught, or not taught, in public or government schools. What a blessing Christian education is for parents who have aspirations of God's will for their children, rather than simply schooling them. What a wonderful option for obedient parents who take seriously God's requirement of them to train their children in the discipline and admonition of the Lord.

It may seem the terms *schooling* and *education* are the same, and even I may use them interchangeably in this book, but they are not: Schooling is the *process* of educating children. In other words, an education is what students receive from their schooling.

Let's begin this book by asking a series of questions every Christian school must ask. Some of these questions have come from parents, teachers, and school staff while I served as a Christian school board member over the years. All of these questions will either be answered in this book, or information will be given so you can formulate your own answer:

- Does your Christian school meet the expectations and requirements of parents who are looking to your school to educate their children as God outlines in His Word?
- Does your Christian school take seriously the responsibilities those parents are placing on you?
- What standards are they evaluating your school against?
- What standards does your school evaluate itself against?
- From a business perspective, what is your "product", what is the "quality" of your product, and what is the "value" of your product?
- What qualities does your Christian school have that will entice parents to choose to send their children to your school over another Christian school?
- Does God give standards, requirements, or even guidelines for Christian schooling? What are they?
- Does God's Word have anything to say about any (or all) of the scholastic subjects taught?
- Does God have any standards, guidelines, or requirements for school administration, teachers, school policies, and discipline?
- Does God give standards or advice on whom to hire as the school Administrator and teachers?
- Does God have standards, guidelines, or requirements for students?
- Is an obedient Christian school safe from troubles, trials, or attacks from the Enemy?
- How can a Christian school recognize the Enemy's attacks and be able to withstand them?
- Does God even approve of Christian schools?

You will notice the word *standard* in many of those questions. It is very important in Christian schooling to understand what that standard is. From the Merriam-Webster dictionary, standard means "something established by authority, custom, or general consent as a model or example: something set up and established by authority as a rule for the measure of quantity, weight, extent, value, or quality:"[7] I am sure you would agree a Christian school is established by God's authority. And, I certainly hope that the model or example used in its establishment was God's Word, the Bible. A Christian student's education should come from biblically based schooling. I also certainly expect the standard now used by a Christian school as the rule of measure or evaluation, extent, value, and quality *continues* to be the Bible. This book will not only explain how, but also challenge your school to ensure and to improve the use of God's Word in all aspects of schooling.

The standard or *established authority* for Christian schools and the resulting education is God's Word, the Bible. It has everything required to be *the* standard. It is the model, example, the established authority by the greatest Authority, and is the rule of measure. One only needs to recognize this, and to know how to use this standard. Subsequent chapters in this book will explain how, including examples, and will give you the confidence in this standard as God wants you to have. God considers His Word the Bible authoritative, and complete. He thinks so highly of His Word that David in Psalm 138:2 said "For You have magnified Your word above all Your name." If you are involved in Christian education at any level, you must set God's Word as *the* established authority.

The Bible must be foundational. Asking questions is essential for growth, change for the better, or keeping on the right track, and of course, those must come with the right answers. First, the *foundation* for those answers must be set in place. In the construction of a building, the foundation is the most important part of the successful structure, quality, effectiveness, and longevity of that building. Likewise is the importance of the *foundation* of a successful

Christian school. You are probably familiar with the Bible passage about the wise man that built his foundation on a rock, and the metaphor used insinuates the rock is Jesus and His Word. Several of the Psalms mentions God as the solid rock and foundation.

The foundation of a building will only serve its purpose well if it has *quality* materials and workmanship. Equally important is how *sound* the foundation is which results from the proper design, taking into consideration the type and size of the structure, and the surrounding environment. Christian education must have a foundation built on quality and soundness, so in the next couple of chapters, those two terms will be explained in detail, and you will see how important they are.

"Education without values, as useful as it is, seems rather to make a man a more clever devil." –C.S. Lewis

Chapter 2

The Significance of "Quality"

The word "quality" means: "a peculiar and essential character: a degree of excellence: ...a distinguishing attribute." *(Merriam-Webster)*[8]. This book will help a Christian school evaluate and/or create their "peculiar and essential character". It will also help the school look at its "distinguishing attributes"; and find what degree of excellence it has. To accomplish these, there needs to be a proven standard to measure against. There needs to be an established statement of what the quality level is expected to be, and there needs to be a manual of procedures to use to achieve and ensure that quality. That standard of measurement in Christian schooling is the Word of God and God's principles. As mentioned in the introduction of this book, you are to keep a look out for individual statements that make up the elements of sound Christian education so here is the first one:

The Word of God and God's principles are the standard of measurements used to evaluate and construct the character and distinguishing attributes of a sound Christian school.

Let me interject a very important comment before continuing: If your Christian school's foundation and policies are not based solidly on godly principles, then please consider removing the name *Christian* from your school. All Christian schools should stand on the same biblical foundation, the same 'Christ'-ian basis, or those that do will consider those that do not to be impostors, denigrating the term *Christian school*, and therefore offensive to Jesus Christ.

Since the term Christian means Christ follower, or little Christ, a Christian school must therefore be rooted in the character and teachings of Jesus Christ. And, since Jesus said "In the volume of the book it is written of me" (Hebrews 10:7), the whole Bible should be used as the standard and basis of Christian school establishment, policies, and curriculum. In chapter 1 of the gospel of John, he establishes that Jesus Christ is the embodiment of the whole Word of God: "The Word of God became flesh and dwelt among us" is what he said in verse 14, so a Christian school *must* be founded, rooted, and based on sound 'Christ'-ian principles from the Word of God. (Specific principles will be covered in detail throughout this book.) That presents a second quality element:

Sound Christian schools are "Christ Followers" and are rooted in the character and teachings of Jesus Christ as the foundation for all aspects of their schooling.

In addition to that, do not, by any means, un-tether *Jesus* from the Word of God. That might be a strange comment, but you realize its validity when you consider that Satan has few issues with teaching laws, ethics, or what we call morality, but he does have issues with Jesus, and he does not want Jesus to be known as the basis of those three things. When you disconnect Jesus from laws, ethics, or morality, as Satan hopes you do, then you have no real and true basis for them. Morality then becomes movable, with no anchor or foundation, and that means morality can change and be different for different people, which presents a lot of problems.

In our world today, we see the detrimental results of disconnecting Jesus from morality: Moral relativism, situation ethics, truth that differs from person to person, etc. Jesus is *the* author of laws and morality, and Christian schools must include Jesus as its anchor or foundation in *all* areas, and especially in the teaching of morals. That is why John began his gospel so very eloquently establishing in chapter 1 that Jesus is the Word of God; there is no separation or difference. Laws and morality must be based on the Word of God, or they don't work. That gives students the correct basis of their beliefs, which is used for their growth in Christ, their life of service to Him, and for the all-important trait a Christian must learn: *discernment.* Discernment is distinguishing between Truth and error, or right and wrong (more on that later). So tying that concept with the term "quality" mentioned above, students must have as their anchor or foundation or "distinguishing attribute": Jesus, the Word of God.

Sound Christian schooling does not un-tether Jesus from the Word of God, laws, ethics, or morality. This becomes the basis for beliefs, growth in Christ, and for discernment.

I believe there are three basic and essential components to the *quality* of a sound Christian school:

1) Using the Bible in all aspects of schooling including evaluation, curriculum, policies, and administration.
2) A true biblical Christian requirement of all school employees.
3) What will be described as the *whole counsel of God.*

Using the Bible

The Bible is filled with passages that say we are to use it for schooling our children. It is the standard for what is right and wrong; it is the standard for basing and teaching laws, ethics, and morality as previously mentioned. It even says why we are to teach the Bible. Paul says several places in Romans that God's laws are perfect, holy, right, and good. Here are a few other examples of what God says about using His Word for teaching students, and remember, these are not suggestions, but commands that require obedience:

2 Timothy 3:16-17:"All Scripture is given by inspiration of God, and is profitable for doctrine, for reproof, for correction, for instruction in righteousness, that the man of God may be complete, thoroughly equipped for every good work."

Psalm 19:8-9: "The law of the LORD is perfect, converting the soul; The testimony of the LORD is sure, making wise the simple; The statutes of the LORD are right, rejoicing the heart; The commandment of the LORD is pure, enlightening the eyes."

Psalm 119:4-16 has these phrases: "You have commanded us To keep Your precepts diligently. Oh, that my ways were directed To keep Your statutes! Then I would not be ashamed, When I look into all Your commandments. I will praise You with uprightness of heart, When I learn Your righteous judgments. I will keep Your statutes; Oh, do not forsake me utterly! How can a young man cleanse his way? By taking heed according to Your word. With my whole heart I have sought You; Oh, let me not wander from Your commandments! Your word I have hidden in my heart, That I might not sin against You. Blessed are You, O LORD! Teach me Your statutes. With my lips I have declared All the judgments of Your mouth ...I will delight myself in Your statutes; I will not forget Your word."

Psalm 119:128 "Therefore all Your precepts concerning all things I consider to be right"

Nehemiah 9:13-14 says that God "... gave them just ordinances and true laws, Good statutes and commandments...And commanded them precepts, statutes and laws"

Hosea 14:9 "Who is wise? Let him understand these things. Who is prudent? Let him know them. For the ways of the LORD are right; The righteous walk in them, But transgressors stumble in them."

When Moses was teaching about God's laws, he said in Deuteronomy 6:6-9 "And these words which I command you today shall be in your heart. You shall teach them diligently to your children, and shall talk of them when you sit in your house, when you walk by the way, when you lie down, and when you rise up. You shall bind them as a sign on your hand, and they shall be as frontlets between your eyes. You shall write them on the doorposts of your house and on your gates."

In taking a look at schooling, how often is the Bible used in the classrooms compared to the above statement from Moses? If you are a parent, how does your parenting compare to this statement? Here is a simple test if you are not sure: Can your students/children recite from memory the Ten Commandments in order? Those most basic laws of God should roll right off of the tongue of every student of a sound Christian school.

Similar to Moses' statement is Proverbs 6:20-23 where Solomon tells parents (and I think teachers also) to instruct children to not forsake the laws (of God, parents, or Christian schools), and to bind them continually on their heart, and to tie them around their neck. God's laws will lead them in life, and will keep them when they sleep, and will talk to them when they wake up. God's laws are a lamp in a darkened world. Are they the lamp in your school?

To many people, God's Word is a concept. They do not move it from a concept to a useful methodical actuality in their life, and that is unfortunate, and cuts short the power of God's Word.

Christian schools ensure the Bible is a systematically practiced reality, not just a concept.

Why Education Should Include the Bible

In the 2 Timothy 3:16 passage just mentioned there are several reasons why the Bible is to be taught in school. It says all Scripture has been given by the inspiration of God and is valuable to use for doctrine (sound teachings), for establishing what is right and wrong as well as what is correct behavior and for pointing out and correcting wrong behavior, positive training of children so they can be thoroughly equipped for every good work. Parents are responsible for that, but Christian schools or home schools also deal with, or do those.

2 Timothy 4 goes on to explain further reasons for including the Bible in classroom subjects: Paul wholeheartedly commands to "proclaim the Word!" He says to do so "in season and out of season", which means in everything, whether it is popular or convenient or not, so find a way to work it in to the subjects taught. He says to "Convince, rebuke, exhort, with all longsuffering and teaching." Yes, he said all teaching (there is no comma after longsuffering which ties the word "all" to the word "teaching"). Then, he tells another reason why we are to include the Bible in all teaching in verse 3: "For the time will come when they will not endure sound doctrine, but according to their own desires, because they have itching ears, they will heap up for themselves teachers; and they will turn their ears away from the truth, and be turned aside to fables." Haven't we all seen that occurring in our society today?! It will be more prevalent when our students grow up. Many people turn away from the Truth, and go to those that tell them what they want to hear, even though it is false, untrue, and fables. Prepare your students to withstand that temptation.

I remember years ago seeing a drawing of a duck, but when you rotate the drawing on its side, it becomes a rabbit. It is very interesting that it can be a totally different image when the base or reference point is changed. Setting biblical Truth as the base or reference point for students is an absolute must for Christian schools. The resulting education students receive must have God's Word as the reference point because their world views, opinions, and outlook on life's issues will come from that reference point.

Education must include Scripture passages in every subject because it is Truth, and because God says so. Teachers and writers of school textbooks must interweave the Truth in all scholastic subjects taught. Paul stated that command emphatically in this way from verse 1 "I charge you therefore before God and the Lord Jesus Christ, who will judge the living and the dead at His appearing and His kingdom: Preach the word!" Teachers, are you obeying that unambiguous command?!

The spiritual life (and sin in it) of teachers and students, is in a direct proportion to the amount of God's Word read and incorporated into the lessons taught.

Having Confidence in the Bible

I hope to have explained how important the Bible is to Christian schooling. I hope you also have *confidence* in the Bible for use in all aspects of schooling, especially when Satan is trying to erode that confidence in Christians by causing doubts. Be aware of those erosion fallacies; do not allow them to creep into your thoughts, or school.

- You should have no doubts as to the inerrancy of God's Word.
- You should have no doubts that God directed and approved of every word.
- You should have no doubts that God has kept His Word accurate through the years. (You should be discerning enough to know which translation(s) are good and which ones to be wary of).
- You should have no doubts that even the letters in the New Testament are Scripture (God's Word). (For example, Peter said in 2 Peter 3:15-16 that Paul's writings were *Scripture*)
- You should have no doubts that the Bible can be used in some capacity in all scholastic subjects.

In addition to your own study of scripture, help from the Holy Spirit, and trust in God, there are several good resources to help you arrive at the needed level of confidence in the Bible: "You Can Trust the Bible"[9] is very good by John MacArthur. I particularly like F.F.Bruce's book "The New Testament Documents: Are They Reliable?" Another is by J. Hampton Keathley, III a Dallas Theological Seminary graduate, pastor for 28 years and teacher of New Testament Greek, who wrote a very good article, which can be found on-line, called "The Bible: The Inerrant Word of God" [10] A portion of this article describes how Jesus taught about the inerrancy and inspiration of the Old Testament:

(1) **Its entirety;** the whole of the Bible is inspired (Matt. 4:4; 5:17-18). In Matthew 4:4, Jesus responded to Satan's temptation by affirming verbal plenary inspiration when He said, man is to live by *every word* (plenary) that proceeds out of the *mouth of God* (inspiration). In Matthew 5:17-18, Christ promised that the entire Old Testament, the Law and the Prophets, would be fulfilled, not abolished. In fact, He declared that not even the smallest Hebrew letter, the *yodh*, which looks like an apostrophe ('), or stroke of a letter, a small distinguishing extension or protrusion of several Hebrews letters (cf. the extension on the letter R with it absence on the letter P), would pass away until all is fulfilled. Christ's point is that it is all inspired and true and will be fulfilled.

(2) **Its historicity;** He spoke of the Old Testament in terms of actual history. Adam and Eve were two human beings, created by God in the beginning, who lived and acted in certain ways (Matt. 19:3-5; Mark 10:6-8). He spoke of Jonah and his experience in the belly of the great fish as an historical event (Matt. 12:40). He also verified the events of the flood in Noah's day along with the ark (Matt. 24:38-39; Luke 17:26-27). He verified God's destruction of Sodom and the

historicity of Lot and his wife (Matt. 10:15; Luke 17:28-29). These are only a few illustrations; many others exist.

(3) **Its reliability;** because it is God's Word, the Scripture must be fulfilled (Matt. 26:54).

(4) **Its sufficiency;** it is sufficient to witness to the Truth of God and His salvation (Luke 16:31).

(5) **Its indestructibility;** heaven and earth will not pass away until it is all fulfilled. Nothing can stop its fulfillment (Matt. 5:17-18).

(6) **Its unity;** the whole of the Bible speaks and witnesses to the person and work of Christ (Luke 24:27, 44).

(7) **Its inerrancy;** men are often in error, but the Bible is not; it is Truth (Matt. 22:29; John 17:17).

(8) **Its infallibility;** the Bible cannot be broken, it always stands the test (John 10:35).

The Sufficiency of the Bible

I hope you also believe that the Bible is *sufficient* for use in Christian life and schooling. (Sufficient means it is enough to meet the needs of the situation or a proposed end). The Bible's sufficiency is something I encourage you to ponder, research, realize, agree, and embrace. Then ensure you parlay that sufficiency into your school's curriculum, statement of faith, handbook, policies, and topics of school assemblies. It should become part of your regimen and become common knowledge among your staff and students. God intends the Bible to be the very foundation of Christian education. 1 Thessalonians 5:20 tells us succinctly to not despise the teachings of the Bible, and that is a very important concept for Christian schooling. Also, don't diminish the teachings of the Bible in your Christian schooling, in fact, that brief passage implies the opposite is true as well: to include and *increase* the teachings of the Bible in your school. You should be *excited* to use the Bible in your school, and look for ways to weave it into all your subjects and policies. There will be numerous practical examples and how to do this in your school throughout this book.

I also want to make sure you understand, and teach in your Christian school that, as John chapter 1 explains, Jesus is God who came and dwelt among us. In the first chapter of Colossians Paul states that by Jesus all things were created that are in heaven and earth, visible and invisible. Also, in chapter 2 that Jesus is everything. Romans 11:36 says about Jesus "For of Him and through Him and to Him are all things, to whom be glory forever. Amen."

Sound Christian schools include the Bible for teaching, and for establishing God's laws, including what is right and wrong, in all their classes and subjects, and believe it is sufficient for doing so.

Christian Requirement

The Christian school's administration, teachers, and if possible all other staff members, must be true biblical Christians. That is, a person who has realized he (or she) is a sinner and that his sins have offended and ostracized him from a just God, he has understood that God requires payment for his sins, which is death. But then understood that if he humbly comes before God and truly repents of his sins, confesses with his mouth that Jesus is Lord and that His work on the cross paid the penalty for his sins as God required, and has given his life to following and serving the risen Jesus, and there is fruit or evidence of that service, then he (or she) is what I mean by a true biblical Christian.

Beliefs of the school employees (administration, teachers, and staff) matter because those beliefs will carry through into their leadership, teaching, and handling of situations that arise such as discipline, policy writing and administering, and various other situations and decisions that come up with students, parents, or others. When parents entrust their children to a Christian school, they assume the policies and the teaching will be based on the "common ground" of biblical standards and principles; they will also assume those leading the school, and teaching in the school, embrace that biblical standard wholeheartedly. You cannot give what you do not have, so if the Bible is not at the forefront of the teacher's thoughts, how can that teacher teach subjects with a biblical perspective?

Please be aware that there are "nice" people, and there are "moral" people who may appear to be true Christians but simply are not, so make sure each person has a salvation testimony and a personal relationship with Jesus. To re-iterate, all employees of the school must be "on the same page", and that "page" is the entire Word of God and obedience to it. Non-Christians have no place teaching in a Christian school, therefore it should be completely understood, and agreed upon, that all employees of a Christian school are to be true biblical Christians, with a testimony of their salvation.

I think the "do not be unequally yoked" requirement of 2 Corinthians 6:14 has relevance here and certainly carries the same principle. Whatever the situation, whatever the discussion, whatever the decision; all can find a point of reference, common ground, or foundation in the Bible. And, since the Holy Spirit that indwells each true Christian is the same Holy Spirit that guided the writing of each word in the Bible, there is wonderful and awesome power in the Bible to base and guide each situation, discussion, or decision if true biblical Christians are involved.

Isaiah 33:6 is a great verse for the Christian school, it sums up very well the Christian requirement mentioned above: "Wisdom and knowledge will be the stability of your times, And the strength of salvation; The fear of the LORD is His treasure."

- The *stability* of your school is directly related to the biblical wisdom and biblical knowledge of your school's administration, teachers, and staff. (Knowledge is things a person knows, wisdom is how to apply those things)

- The salvation of all school employees is the *strength* of the school.
- The fear of the Lord of your employees is God's *treasure* in your school.

How does each employee compare to those three things? Keep them in mind when interviewing people for positions in your school: The salvation, fear of the Lord, and biblical knowledge and wisdom of the candidate should be some of the major criteria of the interview and hiring decision. According to Hebrews 13:7, students are to imitate their godly Teachers: (So make sure your school has godly Teachers!) "Remember your leaders, who spoke the word of God to you. Consider the outcome of their way of life and imitate their faith." (NIV)

Sound Christian schools have true biblical Christians as administrators, teachers, and staff. The stability of the school depends on that requirement.

The Whole Counsel of God

In addition to the aforementioned essential Christian school qualities of requiring employees to be true biblical Christians, and using the Bible as the foundation for policies and teaching, it is important how God's Word is treated and esteemed. Another way of stating this third quality of sound Christian schools is to not purposefully denigrate the Word of God. That may sound a bit inane in a Christian school, but I have seen unintentional misuse of the Bible, which causes great harm. This has been done in various ways, such as neglecting portions of the Bible that are thought to be offensive to some, adding to God's Word to make or support a decision, and passages taken out of their context to say something the Bible really did not say.

Do not disparage (to degrade or depreciate by indirect means), belittle (reduce or dismiss the importance of), or defame (attack the reputation or character by slanderous remarks) God's Word. Maintain and teach the lofty stature and relevance of the whole of God's Word. One requisite is found in numerous places in Scripture such as Deuteronomy 4:2, 12:32, Proverbs 30:6, Jeremiah 26:2, and Revelation 22: 18-19, which is that we are not to add to, nor take away from God's Word. Christian schools can do just that when they either expand on certain passages or themes beyond what is there, or change what is there, or neglect certain passages because of fear of controversy or backlash from parents or society.

Two brief examples that actually occurred in a Christian school I know are:

- A Junior High School science teacher decided to just quit teaching anything on the age of the earth because it was too controversial, and he was tired of arguing with parents who say "real science says the age of the earth is over 4 billion years old".
- The Christian school passed a policy that no one is to mention the word "hell" because it is considered profanity, and also, God would not condemn a creation He loves to such an awful place.

Christian schools should be more conscious of not offending God and His Word than they are of offending people. Dr. Joel Beeke, President of Puritan Reformed Theological Seminary said in an on-line video that you cannot excise certain passages of Scripture, such as the (numerous) Bible references to Hell, because it might be offensive or harsh, or you will deny the whole counsel of God.[11]

The *whole counsel of God* is a concept deserving attention and adherence by Christian schools, not just Pastors or Elders in a church. Christian schools should take the basic elements of the whole counsel of God and weave them into the curriculum of their school purposefully, and with the goal of weaving the whole counsel of God into the training (nurture and admonition of the Lord) of their students. Then, as a result, the *whole counsel of God* should be a part of everyday life of a properly trained student from your Christian School. *Whole* is the key word, meaning not missing any parts. An analogy would be a house that has all the components of the building except it has no plumbing at all. It is still a house, but without water or functioning toilets, it is lacking a valuable component, and is of little use or value. Use every available opportunity to teach all aspects of God's Word to students who are valuable and can be of great use to God.

What are the basic tenements of the *whole counsel of God*? The best and most concise explanation I have found is the brief commentary on the passage from Acts 20:27 by John MacArthur in the MacArthur's Study Bible where he says "The entire plan and purpose of God for man's salvation in all its fullness: divine truths of creation, election, redemption, justification, adoption, conversion, sanctification, holy living, and glorification. Paul strongly condemned those who adulterate the truth of Scripture (2 Cor. 2:17; 2 Tim. 4:3, 4; cf. Rev. 22:18, 19)."[12]

In that Acts 20 passage, Paul was about to leave his three-year ministry to the Ephesians' Church and move on, but before he left, he made his concerns known where he said in verse 20 "…I kept back nothing that was helpful, but proclaimed it to you, and taught you publicly…", and from verse 27: "For I have not shunned to declare to you the whole counsel of God." Then, he explains in verses 28 through 32 why it is so very important to teach the whole counsel of God, and even though this is written to elders in the church, please read this with a Christian school and students in mind, because the same warnings and predictions of Paul apply: "Therefore take heed to yourselves and to all the flock, among which the Holy Spirit has made you overseers, to shepherd the church of

God which He purchased with His own blood. For I know this, that after my departure savage wolves will come in among you, not sparing the flock. Also from among yourselves men will rise up, speaking perverse things, to draw away the disciples after themselves. Therefore watch, and remember that for three years I did not cease to warn everyone night and day with tears. "So now, brethren, I commend you to God and to the word of His grace, which is able to build you up and give you an inheritance among all those who are sanctified." (Act 20:28-32)

If you do not teach the whole counsel of God, then you are warping students by giving them an incorrect idolatrous view of God. Ephesians 4:14 says "that we should no longer be children, tossed to and fro and carried about with every wind of doctrine, by the trickery of men, in the cunning craftiness of deceitful plotting," so it is very important to provide a solid foundation from the Word of God, so your students will not be susceptible or gullible to worldly doctrines that will come along.

I know it is really daunting to teach the whole counsel of God, but that is why it is so important. It is also daunting to explain in this book what that means, or what it looks like in your classrooms. But at risk of straying too far off the topic at hand, I will offer some suggestions anyway:

- Teach about creation, sin and the fall of man, that all people are sinners, God's penalty of sin, God's plan of redemption of sin, the reason Jesus came and died, teach how to be saved, what is a true biblical Christian, what examples of fruit Jesus requires of Christians, teach about hope, fear, love, the character Joseph had, the faith Abraham had, the hope and focus on Christ that Paul had, and what caused Judas to betray Jesus. Use that as the basis of explaining the biblical world view to students.
- Teach how Satan fell, and teach about pride as the root of most all sin. Use that as the basis of why there is laws and

rules, governments, and prisons, or even the economic woes of our country.

- Teach about the amazing grace of God, teach about the Holy Spirit, teach how to find passages in the Bible that pertain to any topic, teach how to discern between good and evil, teach that we do not wrestle against flesh and blood, but against unseen powers, teach how to put on the whole armor of God and what each item of that armor is, teach the greatest commandments which is to love God and to love others (and examples of how to do that), teach to be a servant of Jesus, to obey Him, and to trust Him, teach responsibility and how to have a moral compass.
- Teach that God made molecules, light particles, and why people differ from animals, teach the problems with Darwin's theories, teach about the mathematics found in the Bible, teach the literary structure of Proverbs, and the musical and lyrical structure of the Psalms.
- Teach the sciences found in the book of Job, teach the governmental structure of Romans 13, teach the significance to Christianity of the book Pilgrim's Progress, or the works of CS Lewis, and teach the fulfilled (and yet to be fulfilled) prophecies in the Bible.
- Teach the students' purpose in life is to serve and glorify God, not vice versa, and so the subjects they learn in school are tools they need to accomplish that purpose.
- Teach students to have a hatred for sin, and to have a love for God's Word, and that answers to most of life's issues are found there.

I encourage you to add to that list, and to ensure the whole counsel of God is taught.

Let's flip the coin and look at some examples of what could happen if basic tenements of God's Word are missed:

- If you teach students that God is love, but do not teach about the fall of man, sin, and the effects of sin, then when a student loses a loved one, they may blame God, or may even turn from God because of their lack of knowledge about the effects of sin.
- When you do not teach that Jesus said in this world we will have troubles, but to not fear because He has overcome the world, or that trials are tests and teaching tools allowed by God to those He loves, a student may not handle troubles or trials well or be overcome with fear or worry.
- If you do not teach what the Bible says about topics such as evolution and what the world says about it, your students will not be able to confidently defend their position on those topics.
- If you do not teach and encourage students to serve and glorify God, they will become materialistic, selfish, and self-centered, having an improper view of God.
- If you do not teach the grace and forgiveness of God when a sinner repents, then when a student sins, they may think all is lost, and have no hope.

The whole counsel of God is one of the three most important qualities of a sound Christian school. It is a large and daunting task to ensure it is incorporated in the education of your students, but since I believe it is a requirement of God in your schooling, He will give you the means and tools, the strength and wisdom, and the resources and abilities, to accomplish this quality.

A sound Christian school will encompass and teach ALL elements of "the whole counsel of God", and will not denigrate, add to, or take way any part His Word.

Chapter 3

The Significance of "Sound"

The title of this book contains another significant word to Christian schooling, and may be the key word that unlocks and gains access to successful Christian schooling: it is the word *sound*, which presents a powerful package of meanings. I took the word from Titus 2:1 where Paul instructs Titus to teach according to sound doctrine. Sound means: "Free from injury or disease, free from flaw, defect, or decay, free from error, fallacy, or misapprehension <sound reasoning> exhibiting or based on thorough knowledge and experience, legally valid, logically valid and having true premises, agreeing with accepted views, showing good judgment or sense." (Merriam-Webster)[13]

With that meaning in mind please ask:

- Is your Christian school sound?
- Is your Christian school "free from error, or fallacy" (unbiblical issues or doctrines)?
- Is your school "based on thorough knowledge"? (Biblical knowledge)
- Are all aspects of your school based on the "true premises" of the Word of God?
- Is your school "agreeing with accepted views" of scripture?

- Is your school using good "judgment or sense" when dealing with issues that arise, or when you look for or find some issues that may not be biblically sound?

Your Christian school will be "sound" if your answers to each of the above are:

- We are committed to being a biblically sound Christian school.
- We are committed to being free from error or fallacy. (Free from things that do not line up with scripture)
- We commit to be (and our staff commits to be) biblically knowledgeable.
- We commit to have true premises based on the Word of God.
- We commit to Scripture as our accepted views.
- We commit to discerning biblical Truth from error.

Now, please understand this also: those points imply that the converse (opposite or "other side of the coin") can occur. The Enemy (Satan) will attack your school in various ways, some are subtle, and some are flagrant (more on that in a subsequent chapter). That is why **you must *commit* to the above**. To commit to the above takes work, daily work, a conscious effort of commitment. The school must have a basis to rely on and point to which is the Bible, or school policies that are based on the Bible.

In manufacturing, there are requirements or specifications of a product that state the quality and allowable tolerances of that product being produced. These are the standards the quality of the product is based on and usually point to the National Institute of Standards and Testing (NIST) or a similarly established standard. If not met, the product will be rejected. That standard specifies that the measuring devices used to dimension the product must be based on a gauge block that is certified by their testing agency, and done so once per year to ensure compliance. The perfect standard or "gauge block" used as the basis of accurate measurements and policies in a Christian school is the Word of God.

To briefly expand that concept of complying with an established standard a little further, most Christian schools are accredited or pursuing accreditation. Please ensure that the association or agency of accreditation is biblically sound, and part of that process or compliance includes a periodic review, or audit, to ensure the accuracy and ongoing soundness of your product (the education of students). Also, every several years or so, go through your school policy manual, and your curriculum and textbooks, to ensure they "measure up" to the standard "gauge block" - the Bible.

Knowledge, Understanding, Wisdom

Schools are in the knowledge business. Their purpose is to teach knowledge. But there is so much more than teaching knowledge. Two more items must also be taught in a school: understanding and wisdom. So your school must think, plan, and then do all three purposes as a school in the specific order: Knowledge, then understanding, then wisdom. That sequential order is important, especially when you comprehend the differences of the three. Yes, knowledge, understanding, and wisdom are three different things: Knowledge is the memory learning of things. Understanding is how those things work, came about, and are used. Wisdom is knowing how to apply those things.

> "Knowledge is not enough; we must apply. Understanding is not enough; we must do. Knowing and understanding in action make for honor. And honor is the heart of wisdom." -Johann von Goethe

God promises to give us wisdom if we ask and have faith that He will give it to us:

"If any of you lacks wisdom, let him ask of God, who gives to all liberally and without reproach, and it will be given to him. But let him ask in faith, with no doubting, for he who doubts is like a wave of the sea driven and tossed by the wind. For let not that man suppose that he will receive anything from the Lord; he is a double-minded man, unstable in all his ways." (James 1:5-8)

Notice the negative parts in that passage: people who doubt are like a wave of the sea driven and tossed by the wind, or are unstable in all their ways. What James is saying is that without faith, you cannot have wisdom, and faith comes from learning, which comes from knowledge. So, wisdom can only be given, and it can only be obtained if you have the knowledge. "So then faith comes by hearing, and hearing by the word of God." (Romans 10:17) So, since your school is in the knowledge business, that knowledge must be based on the Word of God. Then, your students will be blessed by God with wisdom.

Proverbs 2:6. says: "For the Lord gives wisdom: out of His mouth cometh knowledge and understanding. Couple that with 2 Timothy 3:16 which says: "All Scripture is breathed out by God and profitable for teaching, for reproof, for correction, and for training in righteousness, that the man of God may be competent, equipped for every good work" (ESV) and you will fully understand that out of the mouth of God comes knowledge and understanding, and all scripture has been breathed out of the mouth of God. The Bible is your basis of knowledge and understanding, which God then uses to impart wisdom to us! I can't resist throwing in one more: Proverbs 24:3-4. "Through wisdom a house is built; and by understanding it is established; and by knowledge the rooms are filled..." Use that metaphorically when thinking of your students. You are like a wise builder and your students are like a house you are building: the "building materials" are understanding and the "furnishings" in the house are knowledge. That frame of mind is definitely a quality of a sound Christian School.

A sound Christian school is built by biblical understanding, and furnished with biblical knowledge.

Why is this so important?

There are numerous examples of failures and destruction of what the lack of knowledge does. Isaiah 5:13 is one: "Therefore my people go into exile for lack of knowledge; their honored men go hungry, and their multitude is parched with thirst." (ESV) Being taken over by their enemies was a result of their lack of knowledge, and God means knowledge of Him and His Word and laws.

Another is written about by the Prophet Hosea in chapter 4 where he reveals God's charges against Israel during one of their worst times as a nation: "Hear the word of the LORD You children of Israel…" (He puts his finger right on the problem of their nation – they don't hear or know the word of the God) "…For the LORD brings a charge against the inhabitants of the land: "There is no truth or mercy Or knowledge of God in the land."" (Hosea 4:1) Their nation was failing, was in horrible trouble because of their lack of knowledge of God's Word. And, in verse 6 of that same chapter, God says to His people: "My people are destroyed for lack of knowledge. Because you have rejected knowledge, I also will reject you from being priest for Me; Because you have forgotten the law of your God, I also will forget your children."

Paul tells us in Romans 15:4 the things that were written before were written for our learning. (Referring to the previous Old Testament passages) What can Christian schools learn from these passages? What can be done to ensure Christian schooling does not fail? As I write this, a news article has just come out where the results of a poll showed that here in the United States of America, our biblical knowledge is at an all-time low. The study reports atheists and agnostics are among the highest-scoring groups on a survey of religious knowledge, outperforming evangelical Protestants.[14]

That study tells us that our pulpits in general, and our schools, yes, even our Christian schools, are doing a poor job teaching the knowledge of God's Word. I am afraid as in the times of Isaiah and Hosea; our country is showing the results of that lack of knowledge. Christianity in America quite possibly is being destroyed because of our lack of knowledge, and if we, as Paul mentioned in Romans 15, do not learn from the Old Testament, then as God said through Hosea, *He will forget us!*

It is the charge, therefore, of *sound* Christian Schools, to teach the Word of God in every subject. Yes, every subject can be taught with some reference, back-up points, or examples from the Word of God, even in mathematics! (Do some research on Dr. Ivan Panin, and look for an article called "God is a Mathematician by Keith Newman).[15] Sound Christian schools should find a way to bring the Word of God into *every* subject.

Parents, you should challenge the school to bring the Bible into each classroom and each subject. You should review the materials used for teaching for biblical references or biblical world views. Visit with the teachers and ask them how they weave God's Word into their teaching. Ask your student if the Bible was used in their subjects that day.

Teachers should use the Word of God as the standard of choosing curriculum materials, as the standard of lesson writing, and as the topics of discussion. Assignments should include research from God's Word, and homework should include biblical passages whenever possible.

Administrators should use God's Word as the foundation for policies, administration, discipline, and it should be the source of your school's purpose. When you review the effectiveness of your school, it should be your standard of evaluation.

Sequential Christian Growth

It is important for sound Christian school leadership to *see the forest for the trees*; to figuratively (or literally) step across the street and look at the school from a godly outside-looking-in perspective. Do this while asking "what is the overall character of our school?", "what do others see in our school", "what do others say about our school", and "what does God think of our school?" Not that the perception of others is an indication of the "soundness" of the school, but it could be with discernment. This is a suggestion from experience because school leadership can get bogged down with responsibilities, tasks, and issues, and can lose sight of the *overall picture* of the school. Maybe you can accomplish this by more tangible means other than perception, such as sending out a questionnaire, or simply asking people you trust to give an honest answer.

One of the best suggestions I can make is to ascertain by the above means if there is a *sequential Christian growth* of the students of your school. Can you see Christian growth through the years a student is attending? Can you see growth continue in graduates of your school? Find out where those graduates are now and ask them what are they doing for the Lord, what is their continuing fruit or growth like? This can be a good indication of the effectiveness, quality, and soundness of the Christian school.

Colossians 1: 9-10 is a great reference to the overall picture of sequential Christian growth in schooling. Each element in the passage can be applied individually to the Christian schools (and students') sequential Christian growth: "For this reason we also, since the day we heard it, do not cease to pray for you, and to ask that you may be filled with the knowledge of His will in all wisdom and spiritual understanding; that you may walk worthy of the Lord, fully pleasing Him, being fruitful in every good work and increasing in the knowledge of God; strengthened with all might, according to His glorious power, for all patience and longsuffering with joy;

giving thanks to the Father who has qualified us to be partakers of the inheritance of the saints in the light." (Colossians 1:9-12)

Prayer is the first endeavor in the sequence. Each day in sound Christian schools should start with prayer. That sets the focus on God, thanking Him for what He has done and given, and to ask Him for the elements of this passage to be brought to the school. Maybe you can write down the elements from this passage for prayer reminders, as well as reminders for your school to do what needs to be done to ensure they are accomplished. Remember, if God wants these sequential elements for your school and students, (and I assume He does) He will give the tools to accomplish them, but you will have to put forth the effort to use the tools, and to ensure these items are sequentially accomplished:

Filled with the knowledge of His will. What knowledge does the schooling impart to the students? Does it include God's will? Is what is taught agreeable to God and His Word? Pray that it does, and then ensure that it does.

Wisdom. Does the school do a good job of not only teaching knowledge, but how to use and apply that knowledge? That is what wisdom is: The application of knowledge. How well are the students applying what they learn? (Can you recognize the sequence forming here?)

Understanding. Paul uses the term *spiritual understanding.* Do students understand what they have learned? Are they able to relate what they learned to spiritual matters? Can they see the handiwork of God in all of what they are learning? Are they learning the ability to apply the biblical based lessons and subjects to the world around them? To serve God with what they learn outside the school? Can they refute error in the world and impart biblical Truth instead?

Walk worthy of the Lord, fully pleasing to Him. Are students well-grounded and confident in what they have learned so that they walk worthy of the Lord being a representative of Him? Are they truly little Christ's? Is God "fully pleased" with the students? Is He fully pleased will all aspects of the school? Pray also for God to show any offensive ways in your schooling as per Psalm 139:24.

Being fruitful in every good work. (Fruit is Christian character or conduct, love of others more than self, humility, giving, praising and thankfulness to God, obedience, good works, generosity, witnessing, etc.) Does the school bear fruit? Or is it on the verge of being cut off as the vinedresser in John 15:1-6? Do students bear fruit? Do your graduates bear fruit and live fruitful lives abiding in Him when they leave the school?

Increasing in the knowledge of God. Are the staff and students more knowledgeable of God this year than they were last year? The attributes of true Christians are being fruitful and increasing in their knowledge of God…does you see that in the students of your school?

Strengthened. How strong is your school? Strength comes with a solid foundation, so how solid is your school's foundation, and what is it made of? This passage says we are to be strengthened and to be mighty with the power of God. Is God the source of the school's or student's strength and might? Or does it come from other sources that may or may not be of God such as material things, wealth, pride, praise from others, or circumstances?

Patience, longsuffering, joy, giving thanks to the Father. These are all attributes that result from the sequential elements listed above. Does the school have those? Do the students?

Taking a hard look at these elements of sequential Christian growth will give you a perspective on how God views a Christian school. Therefore they should be a part of the *standard of evaluation* as to the soundness of your Christian school, and they should be used as goals for the soundness of a Christian school and the students.

> "I charge you therefore before God and the Lord Jesus Christ, who will judge the living and the dead at His appearing and His kingdom: Preach the word! Be ready in season and out of season. Convince, rebuke, exhort, with all longsuffering and teaching. For the time will

come when they will not endure sound doctrine, but according to their own desires, because they have itching ears, they will heap up for themselves teachers; and they will turn their ears away from the truth, and be turned aside to fables. But you be watchful in all things, endure afflictions, do the work of an evangelist, fulfill your ministry." (2 Timothy 4:1-5)

Chapter 4

David's "Letter" to Parents and Christian Schools

King David had a lot of children, and learned a lot over the years of raising them. David had learned some great insights to parenting and we can see some of those by looking at his writings and song lyrics in the Psalms, as well as looking at the life and writings of his most famous son, Solomon. (Solomon was one of the wisest and most successful people in all of history, and through him, came several books in the Bible.) But before we look at David's advice to parents, I want to take you on a little side track from David's wise son:

Proverbs 22:6 is a warning, not a promise!

In the book of Proverbs, Solomon repeatedly tells how to raise and train kids and it always involves teaching godly/biblical knowledge, gaining wisdom from that knowledge, and warnings against ungodly influences. A verse of Solomon we use frequently when teaching kids in Christian Schools and parenting is Proverbs 22:6 "Train up a child in the way he should go, And when he is old he will not depart from it." This verse has become a passage for teachers and parents to put their hope in, a promise to rest on, and a verse of hope to point to when kids stray from godliness. And I believe that is wrong.

I believe this verse is not a promise with a guaranteed return on your investment of biblical teaching and costly Christian education, as it seems to be interpreted in many of our translations, but is a *warning*. The original Hebrew wording of this verse does not have "he should go" but literally reads: *Narrow down your parental training to only what the child wants, and they will habitually do, and recall the approval of, their way, and will not leave their childish ways even when they are old.* It means if parents and teachers are narrow minded and give in to the wicked self-centered nature of children, and don't teach them God's ways which are different than their natural ways, those children will always be sinful, and self-centered even when they grow old. Solomon knew children, and wisely knew godly training was the best way to raise them, or they would grow up always being spoiled, selfish, mostly useless to God, and probably eternally separated from God.

Sound Christian schools don't allow students to continue in their selfish and sinful ways, but train them up in godly ways.

Susanna Wesley, mother of Christian theologian John Wesley, who gave birth to 19 children, wrote in a letter (in which she quoted Proverbs 22:6) the following wonderful comment on training children: "I insist upon conquering the will of children early because this is the only strong and rational foundation of a religious education. Without this both precept and example will be ineffectual. But when this is thoroughly done, then a child is capable of being governed by the reason and piety (godliness) of its parents until his own understanding comes to maturity and the principles of religion have taken root in the mind. I cannot yet dismiss this subject.

As self-will is the root of all sin and misery, so whatever nourishes this in children, insures their later wretchedness and irreligion. Whatever checks and mortifies it, promotes their future happiness and piety (godliness). This is still more evident, if we further consider, that religion is nothing else than the doing the will of God and not our own will.

Self-will is the one grand impediment to our temporal and eternal happiness and no indulgences of it can be trivial, no denial unprofitable. Heaven or hell depends on this alone. So that the parent who studies to subdue it in his child, works together with God in the renewing and saving a soul. The parent who indulges it does the devil's work, makes religion impracticable, salvation unattainable, and does all that in him lies, to damn his child's body and soul forever!"

-Susannah Wesley, July 24, 1732[16]

It is unfortunate that several of our popular translations of the Bible today render this verse the way it is. Other than the literal wording above, a more accurate translation might be "Train up children in their ways, and they will not depart from them even when they are old." I am not saying those translations are wrong, because parents and teachers SHOULD train up children in God's ways, but insinuations resulting from those popular translations can be very wrong. Here are some wrongful results when Proverbs 22:6 is read as translated in most of today's Bibles:

1) If God's ways are taught to children, they will never rebel, and those few that do, will *always* come back to God's ways when they are older, and I think that is wrong. Do you know of any children raised in a godly homes who went to godly Sunday schools and churches or even Christian schools who turned away from those godly ways and never came back to them? I do. And the Bible is full of them. Even in Isaiah 1:2 God's children rebelled, and they all didn't come back to

Him. So I think that makes the popular translation of this passage wrong, and we know God's Word is not wrong.

2) If kids trained in the godly way they should go are godly Christians when they grow old, the praise and glory could go to their parents and teachers who taught them those ways, not in the grace of God and the gospel of Jesus...and that is wrong.
3) If children raised in godly homes where the Word of God was taught, went to biblical churches, or even attended Christian schools turn away from godly things (rebel, become prodigal children, wander away) then that means their parents or teachers didn't do a good enough job teaching God's Word to those kids. It is then the parents' fault: they were not godly enough, or didn't do enough family devotions or read enough Bible passages to their kids, or didn't love those kids enough…and that is wrong. It is wrong because it minimizes the power of sin, the choices each person must make such as their own realization of sin, repentance of sin, and acceptance of Jesus' gospel message. It is wrong because it casts immediate judgment on those parents without hearing their defense.
4) If a child at a young age said a "prayer of salvation" or "asked Jesus into their heart" without personally fully understanding sin and their depravity in it and its required penalty, personally repenting of that sin, and giving their life to Jesus who paid the required penalty for their sins, that child may not be truly saved. Some kids will say that prayer because they just wanted to please their parent, or said the prayer because their friends did too, or maybe did so just to avoid hell (as I did at age 4). They did so their way, but not God's way, and they will go through life with a false sense of eternal security thinking they are saved and going to heaven continuing in that error and not departing from it...and that is wrong.

5) It diminishes the option of God to write that child's testimony, robbing of Him the glory He deserves, and the possibility of winning others to Jesus...and that is wrong. If a program is followed by parents and teachers to ensure godly adults, then the program gets the praise, not the redemptive work of Jesus on the Cross. I have often said, as my own life can attest, that it takes as much grace of God to save a person in a godly Christian home and to keep them saved, as it does to save a person out of a wretched ungodly home. I just don't have as elaborate and astonishing testimony as others may. And I don't care. My testimony may help someone else to be saved and give Jesus the glory, just like someone else's testimony may help someone else. The point is each person must have a testimony of salvation of grace by Jesus, not a testimony of a system followed by godly parents and teachers.
6) It puts the hope of parents into that previously mentioned system of training their children, instead of their hope in the grace of God and the gospel message of Jesus Christ... and that is wrong.

You will see in this book, I repeatedly state that teaching God's Word, and inter-weaving it into all scholastic subjects is THE foundation of sound Christian education. We are commanded to do this as parents and teachers several locations in Scripture. That foundation is needed so the grace of God and the gospel message of Jesus Christ has a place to grow out of and occur. As Paul said in Romans, God's laws don't save, but they point to a need for a Savior. God's word needs to be taught so school kids know of their need and Who fills that need. This Proverbs 22:6 passage says the same thing. It just says it conversely, and warningly: If you let kids have their own way (and we know their way is selfish and many times sinful), they will grow up not departing from those selfish and sometimes sinful ways. They will never know their ways are wrong and a penalty of those wrongful ways must be paid. They will never know that the penalty of those ways, their sinful ways, was graciously paid for on a cross by Jesus.

Sound Christian schools don't make godly students, but lay the foundation of biblical truth from which the grace of God, the work of the Spirit, and the Gospel of Jesus Christ can make godly students.

David's Most Important Psalm

Back to David's "letter" to parents and Christian schools: Psalm 1. It is my opinion that this Psalm was so important that it is placed as the first Psalm in our Bible, and serves as an introduction to the entire book of Psalms. It's principles were undoubtedly used by David in raising and teaching his son Solomon, and heavily influenced Solomon's writings.

For parents who want to have wise and successful children blessed by God. And, for Christian school leaders who also want to obey God, they should carefully study Psalm 1 and apply it to parenting and schooling of children daily. Here is the passage which is in three sections: what *not* to do, then what *to* do, and then the *results*:

"Blessed is the man Who walks not in the counsel of the ungodly, Nor stands in the path of sinners, Nor sits in the seat of the scornful; (2) But his delight is in the law of the LORD, And in His law he meditates day and night. (3) He shall be like a tree Planted by the rivers of water, That brings forth its fruit in its season, Whose leaf also shall not wither; And whatever he does shall prosper. (4) The ungodly are not so, But are like the chaff which the wind drives away. (5) Therefore the ungodly shall not stand in the judgment, Nor sinners in the congregation of the righteous. (6) For the LORD knows the way of the righteous, But the way of the ungodly shall perish." (Psalm 1:1-6)

What NOT to do (from verse 1):

Blessed is the first word, and it is the desire of us all, and the desire we all want for our kids (students): to be blessed by God. We want our kids to have the joy and contentment that comes from being well pleasing before God, and we want our kids to receive blessings from God. It is significant that the book of Psalms begins with the word "blessed", but is especially significant for the context/perspective here, which is a student will be blessed if they obey the verses that follow.

Is the man the term "man" here is the same Hebrew word used in other passages meaning mankind, and so it is not necessarily gender specific, nor age specific. It can be read "blessed is the person who...", or specifically to our topic of study here: "blessed is the student who..."

Who walks not in the counsel of the ungodly, David uses the three positions of an awake person in this sentence (walk, stand, and sit) to express *all your waking moments.* He uses *walks* here to describe an ongoing action for a period of time. That period of time is when children are under their parents' care, nurturing, and training, which in our culture is the first 18 to 23 years of their life. During that time, a parent is to make sure their kids are not in the counsel of the ungodly, which is to also say constantly in the counsel of the godly. Another way of looking at this is if your kids are under the counsel of the ungodly, the passage says they will not be blessed.

Counsel means *tutelage, teaching, advice,* and *influence*, and should not be anything ungodly. (This is one reason this passage of Psalms can be used for parents and education of their children.) All kids' *counsel* needs to be godly, or God based. Who is teaching your kids? Who is giving your kids advice? Who (or what form of media) is influencing your kids? Are they all godly?

Nor stands in the path of sinners, David uses the term *stands in the path of sinners* to mean only one thing in context here: We are not to allow our kids to line up with sinners. The word picture here is of a path with a bunch of people walking in a line on that path. If that path consists of sinners, we are NOT to allow our kids to be one of the people in that path. When there are a bunch of people standing in line, what is going on? A lot of talking, a lot of opinions being said, and a lot of influence. Kids will be blessed by God if they are not hanging around and being influenced by ungodly sinners. Christian schooling should endeavor to provide a full *path* of godly people for students to line up with and be influenced by.

Nor sits in the seat of the scornful; I love this phrase from David; it bursts with insightful instruction for us in our society and education culture today when we study the original meanings of the two key words:

First is the term "seat" which comes from the Hebrew word pronounced "mo-shawb" which means "figuratively a site, and abstractly a session; an abode (the place or the time), an assembly, dwelling, inhabited place, seat, or a situation." (Strongs H3427) So it literally means a chair or desk where people are assembled for a situation or session. Certainly sounds like a school classroom, doesn't it?

The second key word is "scornful". It is important here to realize the term "scornful" comes from the Hebrew word pronounced "loots" and it means "To make mouths at, that is, to scoff; to interpret, or (generally) intercede: an ambassador of derision, to have derision, interpreter, make a mock of, a mocker, or a mocking teacher." (Srongs H3887) The term "scorn" is defined by Merriam-Webster's Online Dictionary[17] as: "**1:** open dislike and disrespect or derision often mixed with indignation. **2:** an expression of contempt or derision. **3:** an object of extreme disdain, contempt, or derision**:** something contemptible." Scorn is a term that is way worse than the meaning of it in our society today, so think of it as the dictionary defines. David equates scornful people as wicked evildoers, and tells again in Psalm 26:5 that we, nor our kids, are to sit with them: "I have hated the assembly of evildoers, And will not sit with the wicked."

So this phrase emphatically means Christian parents are not to seat their kids in any influential or educational situation where there is scorn. To put this passage in a term we can understand today: Christians are not to have their kids sitting in a seat in a classroom where the teacher makes a mockery of the teachings of the Bible (such as evolution, age and origin of the earth differing from God's Truth, humanism, atheism, etc.) We are not to have anyone teaching our kids who openly dislikes, discredits, disputes, or disrespects the Bible. This applies to schools, curricula, teachers, as well as other things that our kids learn from such as some television shows, some movies, some music, some books, or even some friends.

The Bible clearly teaches there are two choices of who we follow: God's system, or the world's system (Matthew 6 is one example), and it teaches worldly ways are generally wicked. Psalm 26 punctuates this Psalm 1 passage by saying we are not to sit with the wicked in any situation where we could be influenced by the wicked. We are to be in the world, but not of the world, to be in the world as light unto the dark world, where light is distinctly different than darkness, and there is no darkness in us. (Matthew 5:14, John 12:46)

What TO do (from verse 2):

After David tells what *not* to do in verse 1, he follows very simply with what *to* do in verse 2. He begins with **his delight**, meaning the person's delight is to incline to, or to take pleasure in: **the law of the Lord**. In the time of David, the Bible they had was the 5 books of Moses called the Pentateuch, which are the first 5 books of our Bible, more commonly known as *The Law*. Today, we are to take that to mean the entire Bible. So we, and our children, are to delight in studying and obeying the Bible.

We can use these first two verses as a litmus test of a child's (or student's) relationship with God, and to gauge their world view. If a child enjoys or delights in doing what is in Psalm 1 verse one, and don't enjoy or don't delight in verse 2, then something is terribly wrong. Aside from the heart of the child, either the parenting is wrong, or the schooling of the child is wrong, or both. We can use these two verses as a gauge of our own spiritual condition as well. If we delight in verse 1, and not in verse 2, so will our children or our students, and then according to the first word in this Psalm, none will be blessed.

David continues by telling us how to recognize those three types of people in verse 1 (ungodly, sinners, and scornful), so we do not engage them as influences or teachers. We do so not only by delighting in the law of the Lord, but on those laws we are to **meditate day and night.** The best way to recognize something as false is to study what is true. It takes a lot of time, energy, and commitment to study God's Word, and the best way to make good use of our time is to weave the Bible into our daily lives, and especially the learning portion of our lives. (Which we all know is ongoing for us all, but is predominantly during schooling years.)

As in verse 1, David uses poetic verbiage to convey frequency, and he is saying here we should meditate on God's Word "all the time". Not just once in a while, as I like to say to students: not just in Sunday school, but in Monday school, Tuesday school, Wednesday school, etc., as well as at home. The Hebrew word for meditate means to study, ponder, and talk. So, all of the time, a person should either *study* God's Word, *think* about God's Word, or *talk* about God's Word. It is vital for this to occur during *all* of a child's learning years. This passage therefore can be used to argue the point that all schooling, including high school and college, should be Christian. As Christ points out in Luke 6:40, "A disciple is not greater than his teacher, but everyone when fully trained will be like his teacher." So parents, who is teaching your child? What is being taught to your child? What teacher will your child be like?

One more thing I want to mention about verse 2 is the Hebrew meanings of *day* and *night* can also occasionally mean good times and bad times. We, and our kids, are to meditate on God's Word in good times and bad. Being blessed by God (from verse 1) is the goal here. Your children will be blessed by God if their education includes God's Word in every subject, and their home life involves God's Word, and done so at all times, including good times and bad.

The Results (from verse 3):

If verses 1 and 2 are followed, there will be a resulting scenario of sowing – reaping, and that is exactly what David tells us by relating kids to a planted a tree that produces fruit.

He shall be like a tree planted by the rivers of water, The first thing to notice in this allegory is someone with intelligence and purpose planted the tree in a place where it had every opportunity to grow correctly and produce fruit. God's plan for a tree to produce fruit is to be planted where it will get all the nourishment it needs to fulfill its purpose. Trees that produce fruit need sun, nutrients, and a lot of water for nourishment. Most apple trees need over 150 gallons of water a week to produce edible apples. By contrast, a desert pine or desert oak needs very little water to grow, however they do not produce usable fruit. In the area that David lived, most all of the trees that produced fruit were planted by people, and were planted next to the rivers. Those fruit bearing trees took in water and nutrients *daily* to maintain proper growth, maturity, and fruit bearing.

As God does so well, this same concept ofTtruth is found in at least one other place in Scripture (important statements of Truth in the Bible have witnesses other places in the Bible). In Jeremiah

17:5-8, God gave His Prophet an important allegory to teach to God's people:

"Thus says the LORD: "Cursed is the man who trusts in man And makes flesh his strength, Whose heart departs from the LORD. For he shall be like a shrub in the desert, And shall not see when good comes, But shall inhabit the parched places in the wilderness, In a salt land which is not inhabited. Blessed is the man who trusts in the LORD, And whose hope is the LORD. For he shall be like a tree planted by the waters, Which spreads out its roots by the river, And will not fear when heat comes; But its leaf will be green, And will not be anxious in the year of drought, Nor will cease from yielding fruit.""

> Notice God says a person is *cursed* when they are trusting in worldly teachings and their heart strays away from God. Then notice God says a *blessed* person is like a properly watered and nourished tree (from God's Word) who will not fear when trouble comes, will not be anxious or worry when situations get tough, and will always produce godly works (fruit) even in those difficult times. Sound Christian schooling *must have that perspective*, and understand that the reasons for teaching God's Word in all subjects in school, and by godly teachers, are to enable the student to be blessed, and to have godly character and fruitful works for Him even in times of trouble. Bible based Christian education is vital!

I have a garden in our back yard at home, and I notice when I do not water the garden with the same amount of water at the proper times, the fruit or vegetables will be small and deformed. Also, those plants that do not get full sun every day have very little (if any) produce. Another aspect is if I do not fertilize the plants or the soil with nutrients they need to grow, the produce will not be very good. So plants need daily water, sun, and nutrients to properly produce good fruit. Just water alone won't work, just fertilizer alone won't work, and just sunlight won't work, but a proper balance of all three.

This allegory of a fruit producing tree, suggests growth and maturity from adequate water and the proper nutrients. The Bible is clear in other passages that people are to grow and mature "to the measure of the stature of the fullness of Christ" (Ephesians 4:13), which includes young people as 2 Timothy 3:15 says: "and that from childhood you have known the Holy Scriptures, which are able to make you wise for salvation through faith which is in Christ Jesus." Also, Peter ends his second epistle with the requirement of growth: "but grow in the grace and knowledge of our Lord and Savior Jesus Christ.", and Paul alludes to teaching and growth in Colossians 3:16: "Let the word of Christ dwell in you richly in all wisdom, teaching and admonishing one another..." Conversely, Hebrews 5:12-14 has an admonishment of spiritual immaturity and lack of growth: "For though by this time you ought to be teachers, you need someone to teach you again the first principles of the oracles of God; and you have come to need milk and not solid food. For everyone who partakes only of milk is unskilled in the word of righteousness, for he is a babe. But solid food belongs to those who are of full age, that is, those who by reason of use have their senses exercised to discern both good and evil."

The first part of Psalm 1 verse 3 says (in light of this Psalm and this book): Godly and obedient parents will place their children in an environment where they will daily learn a proper balance of information and experience, specifically including God's Word and the knowledge of Jesus Christ, to gain maturity by learning how to apply that knowledge, and to use what they have learned for the glory of God in fruitfulness by obediently serving Him in all they do.

Here are a few other things to mention about the fruit producing trees in David's area:

- They did not plant themselves: It took careful thought as to the best place for the growth of the tree and consideration of the future fruit produced. (Parents need to carefully consider where is the best place and/or training for their kids.)
- It took great effort to plant and tend a tree correctly, tilling soil, pulling weeds, pruning branches, fertilizing, etc. (It takes great effort to train kids correctly for proper growth, maturity, and producing fruit glorifying to God.)
- In the arid climate where David lived, properly growing and producing fruit trees were a statement of the skill and effort of the owner of the tree. (What statements are said about your Christian schooling or your kid's growth, and the godly and obedient skills and efforts of your teachers or as you, their parent?)
- Fruit trees were a huge blessing to many people when the fruit was harvested. (How many people will benefit from the kind of fruit your kids produce?)
- Fruit trees were not planted by alkaline or bitter water, or the tree's fruit would not be edible, and of no use to the owner. (You have heard the saying: garbage in, garbage out. What is being taught to your kids during all of their waking hours, and will that nourishment produce godly results that God and others can benefit from?)

I believe parents will be rewarded (or not) by *where* they "plant" their kids because they will one day give an account as to how their kids were educated; and God's Word will be the basis of that judgment. Quality sound Christian schooling is a viable choice for parents to "plant" their kids as God intends. If you are involved in Christian education, please ensure it is biblically sound.

That brings forth fruit in its season. When does a tree produce fruit? In its season. The term *its season* is extremely important here. David could have said "…that brings forth fruit." And ended the statement there, but he did not, he added the line "in its season." (some versions say "in due season") That term is used in the Bible 27 times and always refers to the same thing: that there is a proper and designed period of time for things. Ecclesiastes 3:1 says "To everything there is a season, A time for every purpose under heaven."

When the subject is fruit, a bountiful harvest comes *after* a long and effort filled period of nourishing, tending, pruning, training, and growing, not during. Mark 11:13 says: "And seeing from afar a fig tree having leaves, He went to see if perhaps He would find something on it. When He came to it, He found nothing but leaves, for it was not the season for figs."

David uses the metaphor of a tree bearing fruit in season, in the context and style of Psalm 1, to specifically say that there is a period of time for teaching your kids (watering, nourishing, tending, pruning, training, growing), and *after* that is complete, then they will produce fruit.

When is fruit ready to be eaten? After it has received its nourishment, and is *mature*. Only responsible, aware, and godly parents can tell for sure when their child is fully nourished and mature enough to bear fruit, to be "picked from the vine" and used by God.

Whose leaf also shall not wither; Parents have to be very conscious of the maturity of their kids. If we think they are mature when they are not, the world will overcome them, and they will wither like David says. A withered leaf cannot draw in nourishing sunlight, and the tree does not produce fruit.

Bruce Shortt, author of the book "The Harsh Truth about Public Schools" says that, 88% of children who are raised in Christian homes, attend Christian churches, but attend public schools, will turn away from Christianity. He says that a person's moral foundation is set by about age 9, and the type of world view a person has for life is formed from age 12 through age 18.

George Barna, in his book "Transforming Children Into Spiritual Champions" says that "cultivating a biblical worldview means learning to think and act like Jesus". This means learning Jesus' biblical teaching in every school subject in every school year. Only then, can the spiritually mature person be fully equipped to withstand the Satan led attacks on Christians that come in college, from the secular world, and from everyday life. And, will have the firm foundation to be used by God, and be blessed by God as Psalm 1:1promises.

Our societal laws have placed ages of maturity on some responsible things such as driving, voting, drinking, and enlisting in the military, and I think a child's age of when they are spiritually mature enough to go out into the world and be able to bear fruit (and not be overcome by the world) is similar to those ages, but the Bible does not seem to list any specific age. It does, however, give us this wonderful and perfect metaphor of a fruit tree, and we are to parallel with that metaphor our choices as parents with the focus of our children bearing fruit for God at the proper season.

Proverbs 22:6 says "Train up a child in the way he should go, And when he is old he will not depart from it." When does it say the child will be done with training so he or she will not depart from it? When he is *old*, indicating training takes a long time. The greatest hope for the church, for evangelism, for our country, our world, and for humanity, is in the proper solid Bible based teaching of godly children, who when mature, can unwaveringly act like Jesus and expound His saving gospel *in due season.*

And whatever he does shall prosper. It is when kids have that spiritual maturity, (that ability to think and act like Jesus in everything), that they will fulfill their purpose as a tree fulfills its purpose by producing fruit. In God's eyes, they will they be prosperous in whatever they do, wherever God places them. The Hebrew word for "prosper" used here means to break out on your own, to mightily move forward, to be successful in your trained endeavor. To be prosperous is to have all your child's training in place, so he or she can confidently and mightily move forward with

God's plan for their life. A plan that includes God's blessings as verse 1 promises.

The following applies to Christian school as well as parents, but will be directed toward whom God places the most responsibility: Parents will be rewarded for how obedient to God they were when raising their children. Maybe not necessarily how they turned out, because we live in a fallen world, but in the type and quality of a job they did for their kids in light of God's requirements of them. Generally speaking, how well kids honor God with their life is a direct reflection on you, parent, and therefore your legacy. Please, parents, do whatever it takes, and however long it takes, to correctly raise and educate your child to be **your legacy for God**.

Chapter 5

Choosing a Christian School

Since godly education of our children is so important to God, I want to offer some suggestions for parents choosing a Christian school. The focus of this book, however, is not how to choose a good and sound Christian school, it is on how to be one. So with that in mind, this short chapter can be for the parent as well as the Christian school leader to get a glimpse of a few areas most Christian parents are looking for when choosing a Christian school.

Understand there are differences in various Christian schools, and those differences can be a bit hard to ascertain. Asking the right questions, especially of parents whose children attend the school will help get a good feel for the school. There should not be differences in basic biblical doctrines that a Christian school should hold to, and you will find those core foundational beliefs in the statement of faith of the school. Those are non-negotiable. But there will be differences such as using the Bible in each class or not, school chapel services and what the content is, classes opening with prayer, methods of discipline, teacher qualifications, etc. There are also peripheral differences such as class electives offered, or sports offered. Just remember, core biblical doctrines are paramount and non-negotiable, once you find a school holding to those, then the other or peripheral issues can become the focus of your decision. They become the *personality* of the school.

In comparing Christian schools for our own child to attend, my Wife and I learned some differences in the four schools we considered. (Schools that did not hold the same core biblical doctrinal beliefs as us were not part of the list.) What remained as differences in the schools we looked at were what I would call "traits". Most of these traits came from their founding members, some followed church denomination traits, and some were inherent from the staff. Many of those were overlooked by us, but we ultimately based our school choice on *biblical foundation and Truth.*

We asked ourselves "how did the school handle the Bible?" "How serious are they about the Bible?" "How do they incorporate biblical Truth into the classroom, school assemblies, school policies, and even discipline?" "Do they simply focus on teaching a subject, or is biblical training important too, and how do they do that?" "Will this school train the *heart* of our child in addition to teaching our child's mind?" "Do they require each staff member to be a Christian?" "What are the testimony's of some of the staff and school officials?" "How is Jesus taught and treated?" Asking these questions revealed quite a bit about the schools we compared. I would suggest if you are a Christian school staff member or in leadership at the school, you also ask these questions about your school. Look at yourself from the perspective of a godly parent.

One other thought needing consideration is the will of Jesus Christ. Not only is His Word paramount to Christian Schooling, but so is obeying Him and His Word. Couple with that the wishes of Jesus for us, and you have a well-rounded picture of what a Christian school should be. Just prior to Jesus' death and resurrection, he prayed for us. His prayer is found in John 17, and I am referring to verses 20-26: "I do not pray for these alone, but also for those who will believe in Me through their word; that they all may be one, as You, Father, are in Me, and I in You; that they also may be one in Us, that the world may believe that You sent Me. And the glory which You gave Me I have given them, that they may be one just as We are one: I in them, and You in Me; that they may be made perfect in one, and that the world may know that You have sent Me, and have loved them as You have loved Me. "Father, I desire that they also whom You gave Me may be with Me where I am, that they may behold My glory which You have given Me; for You loved Me before the foundation of the world. O righteous Father! The world has not known You, but I have known You; and these have known that You sent Me. And I have declared to them Your name, and will declare it, that the love with which You loved Me may be in them, and I in them."

In addition to realizing His love for us, you will also notice one of His main concerns and requests to the Father, is that we believers be *unified*. He wants us to be united in the common belief of the Truth in the Word of God. Paul mentions this unity in Philippians 2:2 where he tells the people in Philippi, and to us "fulfill my joy by being like-minded, having the same love, being of one accord, of one mind." That "one mind" he is referring to is answered in verse 5, where he says it is the mind of Christ that he wants in us.

Unity among Christian schools and among the staff at any particular Christian school must be unified around Jesus Christ, the Word of God. Can the Christian school you are considering be defined as unified according to Jesus, and Paul? Later in Philippians 2, in verses 14 and 15, Paul still had unity on his mind when he tells us to be "…blameless and harmless, children of God without fault in the midst of a crooked and perverse generation, among whom you shine as lights in the world,…" Unity is a quality of a Christian school so that outsiders cannot point an accusing, blaming, and harmful finger of accusations of sin or wrongdoing that would damage the school or the cause for Jesus Christ. Unity as described above will enable obedience to Paul's requirement for Christian schools to be lights in the world.

There are undoubtedly countless stories parents of children in Christian schools can tell of the work in their child's life that occurred by the Christian *family of God* that make up the teachers, administration, and staff of their school. These stories bring glory to God. Christian teachers who genuinely care about the growth of students in maturity, well-being, and biblical spirituality are fun to see. Praise God for Christian schooling!

A sound Christian school will have staff and leaders that are unified around Jesus Christ, and the Word of God. Their unity will be evident, even to those not affiliated with the school.

Chapter 6

Understand the Christian School is a Battlefield

Here is a proven fact that can first scare you, then wake you up, then bring you to God and God's Word, which can then excite and empower you: **When a school is committed to being biblically sound, Satan will attack, and try to get it away from biblical soundness.**

A wolf does not attack painted sheep. If "____Christian School" is painted on the building or sign, but very little inside resembles true Christianity (the school is a Christian school in name only), the Enemy will spend very little time or effort on that school. But if the school holds true to God's principles, and Jesus is the school's authority, then it had better prepare for battle. That true "Christian" school will be attacked, or may already be in the midst of one or more. A true Christian school is a battlefield, not easy street. According to Warren Wiersbe "The Christian life is not a playground; it is a battle ground." Since a true Christian school is training Christians to live a life of service to Christ, and to glorify Him, battles come with the turf.

Battles are inevitable. 2 Timothy 3:12 says all who desire to live godly in Christ Jesus will suffer persecution, some attacks are evident, and some are not so evident, but John 16:33 and Ephesians 6:11-12 say you *will* get them. Some Christian schools recognize them quickly, some do not. Some schools have won battles, some have lost them. However, there is good news: as long as you are alive, you can always win back any territory you may have lost in a battle with Satan. Jesus Christ is a winner, and He is an "overcomer" (John 16:33). He defeated Satan's ultimate claim of victory: death, and will defeat Satan in the end. Jesus said He will always be with you (Matthew 28:20), and He will give you strength (Philippians 4:13). With Him on your side, who can be against you?! (Romans 8:31)

How to be Strong

Paul says in 2 Timothy 3:12 that all who desire to live godly in Christ Jesus will suffer persecution. Attacks from the Enemy will come. Count on it. Many attacks will be hard to recognize, partly because no one will show up in a red devil suit or carry a sign announcing the attack, and partly because Satan is crafty, deceptive, and can make lies believable. This book will help you recognize these attacks in the next few pages, but first let's look at what Paul continues to say in verse 13 of the 2 Timothy 3 passage: "evil men and impostors will grow worse and worse, deceiving and being deceived." Christian schools should prepare for those people by being discerning and not being deceived. Be armed for the attack *prior* to the attack (see the whole armor of God in Ephesians 6). Paul goes on in verse 14 to say: "But you must continue in the things which you have learned and been assured of…" He says not to waver from what you know as the Truth, (your biblical knowledge) don't be led astray from God's Word, and *continue* in God's Word. One can be strong, and not waver, when one knows God's Word, and continues to read, study, and apply it.

Take a good look at Ephesians 6:10-20 where Paul tells us we are in a battle with an enemy of God and godly principles: "Finally, my brethren, be strong in the Lord and in the power of His might. Put on the whole armor of God, that you may be able to stand against the wiles of the devil. For we do not wrestle against flesh and blood, but against principalities, against powers, against the rulers of the darkness of this age, against spiritual hosts of wickedness in the heavenly places."

Paul starts out in verse 10 by ordering us to *be strong*. That is great news! We CAN be strong enough to win against the attacks of the devil. When Joshua took over for Moses, he was told by God several times in Joshua 1 to be strong and of good courage, because God was with him. God is with us too!

- We gain strength when we read God's Word, and seek Him.
- We gain strength by trusting Him.
- We gain strength from confidence in Him, the overcomer, who loves us and wants us to defeat Satan.
- We gain strength knowing Jesus is with us always.
- We gain strength when we recognize and thank Him for the character traits He shows us such as love, mercy, grace, kindness, generosity, trustworthiness, etc.
- We gain strength by putting on the whole armor of God (Ephesians 6)
- We are strong when we are like Jesus.
- We are strong when we are confident in His Word, and His promises.
- We are strong when we remember how He strengthened us and was victorious in prior attacks.

Realize There is an Enemy

We tend to minimize Satan and his evil forces. We love to teach that Jesus is real, loving, personable, and relational, but Satan is scary, sinister, mysterious, and evil, so we don't talk about him much.

We may even treat him as an abstraction. He is an idea that we let the Pastor talk about on Sunday mornings, but avoid in Christian education. When the enemy is avoided, then schools play into his hands, and students have an incorrect biblical world view. It is easy for Satan to fly under the radar and hit targets in our Christian schools, and even our student's lives when the radar is not even turned on, or nearly non-functioning. His attacks are much more frequent, much expansive, and I dare to say: much more unnoticed until much damage has been done.

2 Peter 5:8 says "Be sober, be vigilant; because your adversary the devil walks about like a roaring lion, seeking whom he may devour." When you neglect that Satan is real, powerful, and *hell bent* on devouring your school and those in it, you are not thinking soberly, and your lack of vigilance is appalling. You will suffer, and the work of Christ in your school will also suffer.

So what should be done? First, recognize the enemy for who he is, and what his agenda is. In John 10:10, Jesus paints a picture of Satan very succinctly: "The thief (Satan) does not come except to steal, and to kill, and to destroy." Understand your school is a battlefield as previously mentioned, and the enemy is very real. But there is also great hope. Jesus is more powerful, Peter said just prior to his "roaring lion" statement that we are to cast all our care on Jesus because He cares for us (and your school). Jesus said right after describing Satan in John 10:10 "I have come that they may have life, and that they may have it more abundantly. I am the good shepherd. The good shepherd gives His life for the sheep." Then, Peter and also James said we are to resist the Devil and he will flee, followed by this in 1 Peter 5:10 "But may the God of all grace, who called us to His eternal glory by Christ Jesus, after you have suffered a while, perfect, establish, strengthen, and settle you." Wonderful statement of hope!

A sound Christian school does not neglect teaching Satan is a real enemy and on the prowl like a roaring lion wanting to

destroy those who love Jesus, but there is great hope found in the unmatched power and grace of Jesus.

Recognizing Attacks

The hard part generally is recognizing those attacks, or the "wiles of the devil". After all, Satan is the great deceiver, and it takes great discernment, and great knowledge of God's Word to be able to recognize his attacks. Much of the book of Proverbs is how to be discerning; Proverbs 2:2-6, 10-12, 3:5-6, and 14:12 quickly come to my mind where Solomon says: (I will paraphrase here) We are to gain wisdom and understanding, seeking to use those in discernment as one seeks for something desperately needed or as a valuable treasure. We are to seek in God's Word which is where wisdom and understanding come from, and apply those in all discernment which will preserve us and keep us from harm because without discernment, we can fall for ways that may seem right to us, but in the end is the way of destruction.

My Wife was in the banking business as a teller line supervisor. She would train her Tellers how to recognize counterfeit money by having them intently study *real* money. Once they know what the real thing looks like, it is easy to spot the counterfeit. That is a great analogy explaining that studying the Word of God will enable us to recognize what is fake, even if it is just a few words that are not right.

A sound Christian school *can* recognize attacks of the Enemy. Biblical based discernment is the key to doing so, and so is understanding how the Enemy operates so you can, as Paul says in Ephesians 6:11 "that you may be able to stand against the wiles of the devil". Attacks can come in several forms and from many angles in a Christian school, but typically the Enemy will use the same tactics that have worked for him all through human history. One method is to mix in a little false with a bunch of Truth to deceive the gullible or un-knowledgeable. One drop of mud in a clear glass of water still makes the whole glass dirty. The other method is Satan will try to cause doubt in what God says. Here are some examples: "Did God really say…", or "The Bible is antiquated and not relevant to our society today…", or "Surely a loving God wouldn't…", or even "The Bible is too rigid, too offensive, we don't want to offend or scare away people." In schools, one may hear variations of those, as well as people wanting you to "Expand your horizons. The Bible is just one book or idea.", or "The Bible is not a science textbook, science disagrees with the Bible", etc.

I would encourage you to be a *Berean* (Acts 17:10-11) who studied the Scriptures daily to verify Truth. When you know Truth, you will be able to spot error. The opposite of a Berean, is someone who is lazy, ignorant, or close-minded, or self-confident who actually play into the hands of the devil. Those that do not know the Scriptures or do not study them daily are susceptible to attacks and are easy targets.

Sound Christian schools, (including the leadership and staff) must be strong in God's word, to be able to recognize the "wiles of the devil", and are not susceptible easy targets for the Enemy.

Right and Wrong

As mentioned in a previous chapter, God has established what is right and what is wrong in the Bible. The Bible is the authority on morality. God intends His Word to be used as the standard from which laws are based, morality is established, and right and wrong is taught. Part of Satan's scheme of derision and denigration toward God, and to pull people away from God's Truths, includes an effort to convince people that there is no right and wrong, and that there is no morality, only what you yourself establish as right and wrong. Situation ethics (right and wrong can change depending on the situation) is a similar scheme of his, and our society has bought into these schemes hook, line, and sinker.

Sound Christian schools need to recognize these schemes of the devil, and prepare students to defend against them.

Sound Christian schools need to firmly believe and teach that there *is* right and wrong, there *is* a basis of morality, and it *must* come from God and His Word. Recall in a previous chapter the passages that proclaim the Bible as perfect, holy, right, and good? When God's laws are taught to children, they are used by the Holy Spirit to write them on their hearts, their minds, and their consciences, so with His help; they can recall God's Truths when the Enemy attacks what is right and wrong, to the glory of Jesus Christ. (John 14:26)

A sound Christian school will, with the help of the Holy Spirit, write God's laws on their students' hearts, minds, and consciences.

Truth

God is Truth. God's Word is Truth. Just as right and wrong are established in God's Word, Truth is also established there. Jesus prayed to our Father in heaven for us in John 17:17 to "Sanctify them by your truth, Your Word is truth." Christian schools should endeavor to teach God's Truth to their students. I like to capitalize the word Truth because God's Truth is supreme, commands respect, is established, unmovable, authoritative, unambiguous, and unchanging.

"The Truth Project" by Dr. Del Tackett[18] is one of my favorite video series. I would say going through this series is a must for every Christian school or home school. Why? Because in a recent study, the Barna Research Group revealed a statistic that only 9% of professing Christians have a biblical worldview.[19] (A worldview is the framework from which we view reality and make sense of life and the world) That statistic is both shocking, and sad. God's Truth, and how it is perceived in, or related to, our world view, is somehow not getting through to students. It may not even be taught to them in schools claiming to be Christian! If it *is* being taught in Christian schools, it is not being taught in a way that gives students *confidence* in Gods Truth. The Enemy is attacking Truth, and Christian schools need to buck up and fight back with these two: There *is* a Truth that you can know, and what that Truth *really* is. You begin with John 14:6 (Jesus is *the* Truth) and expand biblically from there. Frank Peretti has a great answer for people that may not think there is one Truth: "There is no way for you to know whether what I am telling you is true, unless you know what the truth is. And there's no way for you to know what the truth is unless there is a truth that you can know!"

A sound Christian school will teach their students that there is Truth, and what that Truth is.

> "If you look for truth, you may find comfort in the end; if you look for comfort, you will not get either comfort or truth, only soft soap and wishful thinking to begin, and in the end, despair." –C.S. Lewis

Here is another way to look at this: The world today focuses on our feeling and emotion, but God focuses on our mind, and our heart. He says we are not to be conformed to this world, but to be transformed by the renewing of our mind, so we can prove what is good and acceptable by God's standards, not the world's standards (Romans 12:2). Also, one of my most favorite passages in the Bible is Proverbs 4:23 "Keep your heart with all diligence, For out of it spring the issues of life." We are to fill our mind with God's Truth, and take that to heart, because that is where the issues and emotions of life will come from. Ephesians 5:26 indicates we are to wash, like with water, the untruthful clutter out of our minds with God's Word.

Jesus said in John 14:6 "I am the truth and the life…" Whenever I read that or mention it to someone, I emphasize the word *the*. I think Jesus might have said it that way too: "I am *the* truth, *the* life…" to make sure people know He *is the* Truth. Then, I like to go to John 1 where Jesus is established as the Word of God. Simple, but profound.

We Christians are to fight for, and demonstrate the Truth we believe. It takes a lot of work and effort; repetitious work some times, to get God's Truth into the hearts of children. God is greatly pleased when we make that effort. "Heart work is hard work", is a saying I remind myself of, and you should too. Here is another: "You reap what you sow, so go sow, not just so-so, but know-so."

Sound Christian schooling must include Truth and reality to combat against lies and illusion.

Error

Satan is at war with God. He attacks everything God stands for, everything God loves, everything that praises Him. Understand that simple Truth. It is good versus evil, although probably more accurately stated as evil attacking good. Since Satan is the "father of lies" (John 8:44), error is his best war tactic. US Senator Hiram Johnson is credited with the statement in 1918 "The first casualty when war comes is truth", and that certainly applies to the war Satan wages with God. School leaders and teachers need to remember that we are in a battle, and we need to develop a keen sense of discernment to weed out error, and leave the Truth intact.

2 Timothy 2:15 says: "Be diligent to present yourself approved to God, a worker who does not need to be ashamed, rightly dividing the word of truth." This passage seems to be written to teachers. It takes diligent hard work, being held accountable to God, of which you should not be ashamed; to study the scriptures and make sure

you are dividing the word of Truth. That term *rightly dividing* is the same as *cutting it straight*, which is a construction term of making sure everything constructed is straight and lines up correctly with everything else and has no errors in it. It takes hard work to line the Truth up, and to divide or separate out what is not biblical Truth.

Also notice Christians should not be ashamed for standing for the Truth. Often our Christian teachers take a lot of criticism and verbal abuse because they stand on God's Truth, when the society around them says otherwise. How many have been ridiculed for standing firm on creation and not evolution? How many have been laughed at for standing on the biblical view of a young earth (less than 10,000 years old), instead of an old earth view (4.5 to 5 billion years old)? Christians don't get their praise from this world or people in it, but from God, and obeying His Word.

Sound Christian schools rightly divide Truth from error and are not ashamed of standing firm on biblical Truth.

I just briefly mentioned a few errors that Satan has managed to instill in society that are attacks on God, and in light of the biblical basis of this book, I would like to reiterate them, and add a few more errors that Satan has managed to convince society today as truth. Christian schools should be aware of these, affirm their stances on them, their responses to them, and to not tolerate them. Many of these have come up at the Christian school I am involved in. Along with the attacks, I have taken the liberty to briefly explain *my* opinion as to a response. I believe in the inerrancy of scripture (contains no errors), that it is God-breathed (the very words of God who guided men to write them), and that we are not to add to, or take away from the Bible. I would encourage each Christian school or home school to use the Acts 17:11 principle and research from the Bible to determine whether these things are true for yourself. I have given some scripture references, but you may discover more as you study on your own:

- *Things and life are evolving.* Evolution is a theory, and has not been proven as fact. Christian schools may address evolution, but only as a theory to be made aware of. We are to teach that God created the heavens and a mature earth, for His glory, and for people, and that no creature is evolving into another creature. (Genesis 1:24, Isaiah 42:5; 40:26, Psalms 19:1, 104:24, 115:16, 139:14, Romans 1:20, Hebrews 3:4)
- *The earth was not created.* The ultimate way to thumb your nose at God is to say the earth/universe was not made by anybody, but came about completely by chance. Sort of like if I took an entire week to painstakingly make a dollhouse for my daughter, and she tells everyone it just suddenly appeared out of thin air – I would be devastated. Think about that. (Genesis 1 (God's account) and 2 (Adam's account), Romans 1:18-22, Hebrews 11:3, 2 Timothy 4:1-4, 2 Peter 3:3-6)
- *Flood of Noah is only a Sunday school story.* There was a great flood caused by God as a judgment on the rampant sinfulness (and some scholars say to possibly erase demonic causes genetic impurities of some people), with the exception of a small group of people, and creatures, whom He saved in a large boat. The evidence of this flood is everywhere, but much of it is erroneously explained by greatly exaggerating the actual age of the earth. (Genesis 6 and 7)
- *Adam was not a real man.* Recently, there has become some erroneous skepticism as to whether or not Adam was a real person. There are varying views of this, but mostly they center around the thought that Adam was a description or fictitious and used as a metaphor. The people that bring this error usually are the same people that disagree with the bible's age of the earth. Jesus referred to Adam as a real person, so that settles it, unless you don't believe Jesus.

- *People are basically good.* The Bible teaches that people are born with a sin nature, and are totally depraved. That is pivotal to how education and discipline are used in raising children. The lie of Satan which is the direct opposite of scripture is that people are basically good, and from that error, say spanking (the biblical form of discipline) is child abuse, and will harm the child, or teach children to hit others. That lie is part of a successful scheme of Satan to harm Gods most prized creation: people, and to tear down society, families, and relationships. In other words, his lie says that since people are basically good, then discipline will harm the child, and hurt their self-esteem. The Bible says that people are basically sinful and bad, and if that nature is not corrected by specific discipline, the child will turn out bad, sinful, break laws, and take down other people, including families, as well. Charles Manson is an example of what the lack of discipline and lack of biblical teaching produces. (Psalm 51:5, Jeremiah 4:22, 1 Peter 1:14-16, Romans 8:5-8; 13:14, Ephesians 2:3-5, 1 Peter 2:11, Galatians 5:16
- *God is not one.* This has many differing views. Some say God is actually three Gods, not one in three forms, or that God manifests Himself in one of the three forms or another, but not all at once (called Modalism). Others say there are many gods, not just one (such as the ancient Greeks). Still, others say we can become God, and that God was once a man (Mormonism). Another is that there is no one God, but God is in everything such as the trees, rocks, cows, etc. (New Age, or Hinduism), or that people are their own God (Humanism). There is only one God, eternal, in three persons: Father, Son (Jesus), and the Holy Spirit. (Romans 1:25, Mark 12:32, 1 Corinthians 8:6)
- *There are many ways to God.* Jesus said in John 14:6 "I am the way, the truth, and the life. No one comes to the Father except through Me." So there is only one way to God, which

is through Jesus and all that He said and requires. Everything else is a lie from Satan. (John 14:6, 1 Timothy 2:5)

- *Science trumps the Bible.* Too often, science tries to explain things without acknowledging God, and when it does this, it can only settle on the most believable lie. You can only believe the age of the earth as less than 10,000 years if you believe God, if you do not believe God, then you have to age the earth at billions of years old. Billions of years are a replacement for God, an affront to God's glory, and can confuse those seeking God for salvation; all three are a brilliant scheme of lies by Satan. Christian schooling needs to take this approach: *If science and the Bible disagree, then science is wrong.*
- *Money is the key to happiness.* Materialism is a scheme of Satan to get us away from God's promises of meeting our needs, and to get us away from the true meaning of happiness – serving Jesus, and the victory over death we have and of spending eternity with Him. (Matthew 6:19-34, Luke 18:18-23)
- *It is not your fault.* Satan has brilliantly put the notion in society today that we are not accountable, nor responsible for our actions. That someone else is at fault, or a disease is the cause. This lie can be very aggravating in Christian schools in many areas, including homework deadlines, grades, discipline, sports, etc. Christian schools need to teach accountability and responsibility to their students, and be prepared to teach them to parents as well. An example of this in our society today (which always makes me laugh) is when I see in the news about a vehicle crash and they say "the car went out of control", a deceptive lie that says the driver was not responsible for the accident. Be aware of terms such as disease, or addiction to wrongfully explain away a sin, or shift responsibility away from one's self as if the sinful behavior is a medical or physiological issue.

> Satan also tries to keep from our thoughts that we will have to give an account for what we have done. (Romans 14:12, Matthew 12:36, and many other passages) Another example is "it's not his fault; he is a product of society", or "He had a rough childhood with bad parenting, so he is not responsible for breaking the law". God holds us accountable, and responsible, to diminish that in any way is calling God a liar, and is an affront to Him. To not teach accountability and responsibility to students in our Christian schooling is following Satan's lie. (Genesis 3:9-19, Deuteronomy 24:16Hebrews 9:27, Romans 14:10-13, Ecclesiastes 12:14)

This is not a comprehensive list, but a few items to make you aware of the attacks by Satan, and for you to develop your own list, stances on them, and responses to them. Remember, Jesus validated many of the issues above by quoting, or referring to such items as the flood of Noah, Jonah and the big fish, Adam, creation, Satan, sin, and many others. So if Jesus knew them as literal and as fact, you either have to believe them because you believe Jesus, or call Jesus a liar, and therefore the whole Gospel as a lie. (Wouldn't that make Satan happy?!)

A sound Christian School has a keen sense of discernment able to accurately distinguish between Truth and error, and can spot the errors brought forth by Satan, and not teach them as fact or Truth, or even as the best theory. (Matthew 18:6)

Accusations

The Enemy will bring accusations against the Christian school, staff, or parts of your school's policy. These accusations will come from all angles, and may even come from trustworthy people. A sound Christian school will generally use the following steps when an accusation arises, and if the accusation involves sin, they follow the principles and sequences Jesus laid out in Matthew 18: Listen to the accusations one-on-one. If possible, encourage the accuser to discuss the issue with the person the issue is with, such as a parent meeting with the teacher. If a resolution cannot be met, then meet with a few more staff members, which may include the Administrator. Accusations should not be brought in front of the Board of Trustees unless the prior sequences have not come to a resolution. Be mindful of when to use the Matthew 18 principles which are for dealing with sin. Jesus' process can be used for most accusation, but not all. Many times His process is overused, misused, or even lazily ignored to the detriment of communication, holding each other accountable, and harming the school.

Not all accusations come from the Enemy; some may come from well-intentioned or uninformed parents or others. The Christian school should carefully weigh the accusation against what the school policy says. Draw a conclusion as to what policy the accusation is addressing, or define what the accusation is and then determine what policy it relates to. Depending on the situation of course, I suggest telling the accuser you need time for study, discussion, and a resolution, and then give a time to re-convene. An example would be: "Now that we understand your issue, we will look at it more closely, and get back to you next Tuesday with our position." Remembering that patience is a virtue of God and godly people, so if possible, end the discussion to give you time for consideration. Many accusations loses validity if the accuser is not willing to allow time for consideration and a resolution.

What if an accusation or attack has no policy pertaining to it? Remembering Romans 8:28 that all things work together for good to those that love the Lord and are called according to His purpose, view this as an opportunity for the Lord to work for good in the Christian school. This may mean you need to go through a process to determine if a new policy is merited. So go through the school's process of information gathering, review, and if needed, enacting a new responsive and responsible policy. Carefully consider including the accuser in the policy discussions if appropriate. Always consider the biblical viewpoint as the main source of resolution.

Guidelines To Follow

During a time of accusations and attacks, the leadership of the Christian school may decide a specific issue is serious enough, or has ramifications of such a nature, that you will want to use a specific *process* to work through the issue. Here is a suggested basic guideline or process to follow for the people of leadership taking on this accusation:

1) **Pray**. Focusing on God, ask Him for wisdom, clear understanding of the issue, recollection of Bible verses that pertain to the issue, clear understanding of those verses in His Word, clear resolution based on His Word, and a love for the accuser and that you portray that love to the accuser as Jesus would.
2) **Take time to consider the topic of discussion.** Gather information from all sides of the issue for review. Be disciplined to do this, it takes effort, and also portrays the nature of a fair and impartial judge. Give yourself un-interrupted time to consider the gathered information on the issue. If you are the one person dealing with the issue, close your office door and deal with it. If merited, schedule time with one or more of the school's staff that are involved with the issue, or possibly one or more members of the schools Board of Directors for their viewpoints if needed. Remember, this is the *information* stage, not the counsel stage (which will follow).

3) **Discover the root of the problem.** Does it stem from a misunderstanding? Does it come from immaturity? Ask if this could be an attack from the Enemy. Ask if or what sin this issue has arisen from (pride, selfishness, hatred, lack of respect for authority, covetousness, etc.). You may have to dig deep to uncover a specific sin that is the root of the issue. You could conversely discover the root of the issue is not sin, but that there is no policy or rules governing the issue.
4) **Keep proper perspective.** Satan loves to shrink our world down to the latest problem, so we focus on that only, and then he hopes we will become discouraged and downtrodden with that problem. Don't fall for that tactic. Keep your perspective on the *big picture* as God sees it, and your purpose to glorify Him, and uphold the mission of your school. Don't let one problem rob from the other efforts you have going. Keep in mind the significant as you work through the trivial. Focus on the everlasting as you deal with the momentary.
5) **Worship.** This may be very hard to do, but worship God through all aspects of this problem. That helps keep your proper focus, keeps you humble, and reminds you of the attributes or character of God such as being merciful, gracious, trustworthy, loving, kind, just, and wise. Also reflect on how He has brought you through similar situations in the past. God has a purpose for this trial, so look for it, or look for ways He can use it for your good (Romans 8:28-29). Job had his world come crashing down in one day, and it says in Job 1:20, he fell to the ground and *worshiped.*
6) **Consider solutions (if any).** Remember the Bible is solid and foundational. Your school policy is probably solid and foundational. Your staff is probably solid and trustworthy. Use reliable sources such as these to come up with several solutions. Narrow them down, and settle on the best one.

7) **Envision or "play out" the results of those solutions.** Maybe make a list of pros and cons of the solution. Ask "what would be the result if we…"
8) **Study the Bible for God's answer.** Use a topical bible, or similar method of helping find passages relating to the issue, or the root cause/sin of the issue.
9) **Consult counsel if needed.** God says a wise man seeks godly counsel. Does the situation require Legal counsel? Pastoral counsel? Possibly discuss the situation with the leadership of another Christian school, as they may have already dealt with a similar issue.
10) **Keep it simple, and keep it biblical.**

Keep it Simple, and Keep it Biblical

I always suggest to people facing situations that could be an attack from the Enemy or a temptation of some sort to *keep it simple, and keep it biblical.* All accusations should always be answered with Scripture. When Jesus faced accusations or temptations from the Enemy in Matthew 4:1-11, he always answered by quoting the Bible. God's Word is profitable, reliable, authoritative, and truth. It is able to diffuse a situation about to explode, or provide unarguable support for a godly response. With concordances, topical Bibles, and electronic search tools, it only takes a few minutes to find scripture passages applicable to the situation. Be diligent and discerning, contextually accurate and relevant, and give yourself ample time to let the Holy Spirit speak through His Word. Then, keep it simple, to the point, and draw that point to scriptural support.

You cannot go wrong if you keep it simple, and keep it Biblical.

In the book of Psalms there occasionally is the word "Selah". That word is sadly not part of our English vocabulary. Maybe you can make it a common word in your life, and your school. It literally means *to pause and ponder it.* Whenever you are dealing with a situation and you keep it simple and keep it biblical, remember to also *Selah.* It is amazing the peace, strength, and wisdom God will give you when you "be still and know that I am God", and take a few moments to pause, ponder, and think about the Bible passage at hand, and relate it to your situation with wisdom.

When Joshua was taking over as the leader of Israel after Moses God knew he would be facing a lot of battles and rough times, so God told Joshua to "Be strong, and of good courage!" I suggest the same to you. Be strong and of good courage, which God will help you with if you ask Him, and believe that He will. One other suggestion is to never let the Enemy win any battles. Resist him and he will flee. Never give up doing the right thing, never give up sticking to God's Word and His principles, and I mean NEVER EVER give up!

Know How the Enemy Works

Learn to recognize the attacks of the Enemy: Ephesians 6:11-13 says we will get specific attacks from the devil that we must recognize, and be able to stand against them. Some attacks will be direct, and some indirect. Some will come from within, and some from without. Then, in verses 14-20 Paul tells us how to stand against those attacks by using the WHOLE armor of God.

How Satan attacks the Christian or Christian school is something to know or learn. You must be able to recognize Satan's tactics and schemes to combat his attacks. He is crafty, sneaky, and he is not fair. However, he does use basically the same typical strategies today as he did in the Bible, and he works on or through our weaknesses, so knowing his tactics then will give us an upper hand in defense today. These can pertain to the Christian school, as well as your personal Christian life:

- In Genesis 3, Satan came in a form that did not scare Eve away. Satan or his cronies do not come with a sign around them saying "BEWARE". He is the master deceiver, and will entice our senses to gain our attention. He is wise and subtle, so stay alert.
- Also in Genesis 3, Satan used this tactic on Eve, and it has worked on people ever since: He caused her to doubt what God said. This comes in many ways today such as "Did God really say…", or "Surely a loving God would not…", or "God didn't mean that literally…". even "Surely God wouldn't judge you for that…", or maybe "Most Christian parents don't think that is wrong." To stand up against these, know your school policies well, and stick to them. Know the Word of God well, memorize it to keep it in your heart, and stick to it. Satan loves to cause us to doubt God's provision, God's goodness, God's plan, God's timing, God's promises, and God's Word. A little bit of doubt is like a small seed fallen in a small crack in a sidewalk, that eventually can grow to a plant that breaks up the concrete and ruins the sidewalk.
- Satan adds a little bit of lie to a lot of Truth. The most believable lies are those that have a lot of Truth mixed in. Satan twisted what God said to Adam and Eve just enough to get Eve to stray away. Satan loves to use scripture, but he either changes it just a bit to entice the gullible and unknowing, or he uses scripture out of context to say what it does not really say. In doing so, he promotes his agenda and causes us to doubt or to sin. One small drop of food coloring in a tall glass of clear pure water will color the whole glass of water.
- Satan played on Eve's emotions and got her to sin. Be aware of that tactic, because playing on our emotions is an easy attack that works more often than any other. Our minds are to control our emotions, not the other way around. Stand firm on what you know. Don't fall for what you feel.

- Satan coerces you to believe you can be like God. This is a classic New Age religion tactic that Satan started with Eve. He told Eve "You will not surely die. For God knows that in the day you eat of it (the tree God prohibited Adam and Eve from eating its fruit) your eyes will be opened, and you will be like God." Playing on the pride that is in people to get them to believe they can be supernaturally better than they are, is a worldly tactic of Satan. We are wretched depraved sinners, and the only way we can become anything better, is through faith and trust in Jesus. But, we can never be, or be like God.
- Satan tells you sin is not that bad. When God talked with Cain in Genesis 4, He said "Sin is crouching at your door. It desires to have you, but you must master it." Before we can master sin and the attacks of Satan, we must know how it compels to control us. We must know that sin separates us from God, and condemns us to hell. We must develop an intense hatred for sin, and teach that to children.
- Satan blurs the reality of sin. He may even convince people what God calls sin in the Bible, is not really a sin. He does this by changing the words our society uses to describe sin, or remove all together the ideas that something is a sin. He also causes our society to take the responsibility for sin and push it onto others, or even label specific sins a "disorder". A few examples are alcoholism or drug addiction is now called a disease. Homosexuality or sodomy is now called alternative lifestyle. Fear, doubt, worry, and anxiety are now called panic disorder or bi-polar disorder. Adultery is now called having an affair or experimentation. Be aware of word changes, or labels that mask what God calls sin. Be aware society today even glorifies what is an abomination to God. Isaiah 5:20 says woe to people who do that, and we need to stand firm with God on what He calls sin.
- Satan knows our weaknesses. I believe that we all have a propensity to sin in one certain area, and Satan knows that

area in us, and gets us to stumble in that area whenever possible. For some, that is lying, for some it is worry, for others it is selfishness, or lust, or complaining, but we all have at least one of those. We are to teach students about that in us and that people should identify that weakness and guard against Satan's attacks there. Pray that God gracefully gives strength in that area, and the ability to recognize an attack there before it causes us to stumble.

- Satan plays on our pride. This was mentioned previously, but needs its own bullet point. "You deserve a break today" is a famous slogan of McDonald's Restaurants, and it always would make me laugh. That slogan is the same as one of the devil's tactics: playing on our selfishness. Satan knows pride very well; it is what got him in trouble initially. Teach your students about the fall of Satan (Lucifer) form Ezekiel 28:11-19, and then from Isaiah 14:12-15. Look for the instances of pride, count the statements like "I will…" You will see why I think pride is the root of all sin. Pride started with Lucifer there, and continues today as the main cause of stumbling and sin. Materialism, covetousness, and our wishes or desires are part of this tactic. Not being content with what God has given us is also part of this. Philippians 4:11 is a good passage that teaches us to be content with what God has given us, because of we are not, we claim we know better than God does, or are not happy with God's blessings.
- Watch your thoughts. All sin starts with our *imagination*. Therefore, we are to control our imagination and not allow our sinful nature to control our thinking. I am not sure if Satan is able to place bad thoughts or desires in our mind, but I do know our sinful nature will, if we let it. Teach that to students, so they can be watchful of what they are thinking of, and to have the self-discipline to stop that kind of thinking. James 1:14-15 is a good passage about this, as well as several Proverbs.

- Satan wants to keep you away from God's Word. If he cannot do that, he will cause you to not get all from the Bible that God has there for you. So *study* God's Word. Satan hopes you will just *skim* a particular Bible passage instead of studying or meditating on it. He will do that by convincing you there is not enough time to study the topic or passage. He will also cause you to become distracted and not focus on God's Word. Another tactic is to have you take a passage or Scripture reference out of context, which causes the meaning to be distorted, shallow, or completely wrong. You may recall that many of the Psalms end with the word "Selah", which means pause and think about that. Take that approach to all scripture passages. Pause and ponder what you have just read, and think about what God might be saying to you. Also look up other passages that are similar, but maybe said a different way. Or find the key words in a passage and look up the original Greek or Hebrew meanings to get a deeper understanding of God's meaning. A good study Bible helps with those.
- H.A.L.T! Use this acronym when teaching the tactics of Satan and when he will use them. Satan will attack and has a good chance of winning when we are Hungry, Angry, Lonely, or Tired.

There are other tactics Satan uses to attack us, or cause us to sin, but these above are proven ones he has used for centuries. If you teach these to Christian school staff or to students, please also remember to convey that that Jesus overcame Satan's temptations by using scripture. He also overcame Satan when He rose from the grave. Therefore we can overcome Satan through the use of scripture, and strength from Jesus. So, a sound Christian school teaches how Satan attacks, and by using scripture and strength in Jesus can resist the devil until he flees. Paul taught in Ephesians 6 that we are in a battle, and gave us tools (and a wonderful metaphors to remember them) to battle the Enemy and make his attacks ineffective. I encourage you to study that passage on the whole armor of God, and if you are a teacher, teach it to your students. Those tools are all defensive items except one, which is both a defensive and offensive item and that is the sword – the Word of God. We Christians should put on the whole armor of God to fight the battles, and remember to put on the armor *before* the battle, not during one. So **a sound Christian school teaches the use of the Whole Armor of God to stand against the attacks of the Enemy.**

Preparation for Physical Attacks

On Saturday night August 25th, 2012 a malicious arson broke into Heritage Christian School in Bozeman, Montana and set the place on fire. This was just a few days before school was scheduled to start for their 30th year. The school Administration and Staff found out in a real hurry how prepared they were (or not) to handle a physical attack.

Crime scene tape was quickly strews around the entire school campus by law enforcement and a Sheriff's Officer was stationed at the school to ensure no one crossed that tape. Fire investigators told school officials the next morning they would not be allowed into the school "not even to retrieve a pencil", for up to 18 months due to the ensuing investigation of the crime. So having to deal with the reality of beginning school for 160 students with virtually nothing, not even a list of students or their parents' contact information, class schedules, or textbooks, the folks at Heritage Christian School learned several valuable lessons, and I hope those lessons are taken to heart and action by you and your Christian school. How prepared is your school for such a tragedy? Here are some suggestions:

- Review your school alarm system, and ensure it is working properly, adequate, up to code, and install surveillance cameras if appropriate.
- Back up all of your computer files frequently, and store that back up off-campus. Include all student and parent contact information.
- Do an inventory of school property. Video inventory is simplest, and store the recording in a safe place, possibly a copy of it off-campus.
- Visit with your insurance company and discuss "what if..." scenarios such as what happened to Heritage Christian School. Make sure you are adequately covered. The insurance company and the policy the school had become a real blessing to Heritage.
- Check to see if your insurance company will cover the basic costs of relocating the school if something like the above was to take place, and how much would they cover. Decide on a dollar figure if you have to immediately rent a facility, purchase all new textbooks, computers, desks, whiteboards, etc. Think that one through and make sure you are covered.
- Have a location(s) in mind to relocate your classes temporarily.
- Teachers should have a priority list of minimal things they need to continue teaching off-campus temporarily, and store that list off-campus or on the school computer's back up file.
- Have a fire proof safe or storage box to keep irreplaceable documents and other items in.
- Make bank deposits daily. Don't leave checks or cash in a place that could be destroyed by fire over night; or stolen.
- Make sure your school is "up to code" by asking a Fire Marshal to inspect your school. Remedy any issues immediately.

- Rehearse fire drills regularly, and have escape routes clearly marked in each classroom and office, and make sure each student knows the way out in case of a fire or emergency.
- Keep chemicals, or other accelerants or explosive materials in fire proof containers.
- Have the builder of the school, janitor, or someone who knows the building very well available for quick contact to offer help and advice to the emergency responders.
- Make sure fire lanes are clearly marked and unobstructed so emergency vehicles have easy access to the building, and to fire hydrants.
- Remember a fire causes damage, but smoke and water damage (from the fireman trying to put out the fire and prevent it from spreading) often causes much more damage. Think of how you can mitigate smoke or water damage. Storing textbooks and other materials in cabinets or closets up off of the floor is one suggestion.
- Develop a contingency plan of organization and operation should a tragedy occur. The plan should include one location for pertinent information such as the school web site or blog, a phone number (cell phone) to use if the school phones are not working, a bank account for emergency funds or for people to donate after a tragedy, an office location and computer to upload and access the backup files of the school, people to be responsible for assigned tasks such as running the school web site for up to the minute information communication, coordinate donations, answering calls on the emergency phone, organizing school materials for each class, etc.

God is amazing, and prepared Heritage Christian School in many areas for this tragedy, but remember, we live in a fallen world where sin occurs and bad things can happen, and even though God is in complete control, He can allow those things to happen for many reasons. God has used the tragedy at Heritage Christian for His glory in amazing ways, and there are wonderful stories of school unity, generosity, blessings, and witness opportunities, but I can't help but think other Christian schools can learn and be better prepared if such an event should occur to them. Preparation is part of the wisdom God gives us, if we are disciplined enough to use it.

A sound Christian school prays for God's gracious hand of protection and safety of their school, but also wisely prepares for tragedy.

Chapter 7

Paul's "Letter" to Teachers and Christian Schools

Under the inspiration of the Holy Spirit, Paul wrote a letter to Titus instructing him on leadership in the church on the island of Crete. Quite a bit of chapter 2 verses 1-15 has relevance and value to Christian schools. Teachers and school administrators can apply so much of this passage to their efforts of educating students that it seems Paul was also writing it to them:

"[1]You must teach what is in accord with sound doctrine. [2]Teach
the older men to be temperate, worthy of respect, self-controlled, and
sound in faith, in love and in endurance. [3]Likewise, teach the older
women to be reverent in the way they live, not to be slanderers or
addicted to much wine, but to teach what is good. [4]Then they can
train the younger women to love their husbands and children, [5]to
be self-controlled and pure, to be busy at home, to be kind, and to
be subject to their husbands, so that no one will malign the word
of God.

[6]Similarly, encourage the young men to be self-controlled.
[7]In everything set them an example by doing what is good. In
your teaching show integrity, seriousness [8]and soundness of
speech that cannot be condemned, so that those who oppose you

may be ashamed because they have nothing bad to say about us.
9Teach bondservants to be subject to their masters in everything, to
try to please them, not to talk back to them, 10and not to steal from
them, but to show that they can be fully trusted, so that in every
way they will make the teaching about God our Savior attractive.
11For the grace of God that brings salvation has appeared to all men.
12It teaches us to say "No" to ungodliness and worldly passions,
and to live self-controlled, upright and godly lives in this present
age, 13while we wait for the blessed hope—the glorious appearing
of our great God and Savior, Jesus Christ, 14who gave himself for us
to redeem us from all wickedness and to purify for himself a people
that are his very own, eager to do what is good. 15These, then, are the
things you should teach. Encourage and rebuke with all authority.
Do not let anyone despise you." -NIV

The first section of the scripture, in the light of qualities of sound Christian education, refers to the requirements of Teachers, Staff, and their Board of Trustees. Let's unpack each verse in this passage and apply each of Paul's statements to sound Christian schooling:

What You Must Teach (From verse 1):

"You must teach what is in accord with sound doctrine"

- ***Sound doctrine* means Truth.** Understandably the Bible is Truth and is sound doctrine, and a Christian school must make sure their policies *and* curricula are sound according to God's Word. They must line up with biblical teaching. Each subject must be taught as if an extension of the Bible. Not an addition *to* the Bible, but an extension *of* the Bible.

Each subject, activity, and policy must include the Truths of the Bible. That can be a bit difficult for some subjects but entirely possible (consider that a challenge if you are a Teacher). For activities such as sports, drama productions, concerts, debates, etc., it takes creativity to find ways to bring in biblical passages, values, or principles, but can be done. For administration and all school policies, it definitely *should* be done. Conversely, entering false doctrines into subjects or policies (masquerading as Truth) is detrimental to sound teaching, so beware of that, and beware of Satan sneaking in un-sound doctrines. Remember, Satan uses a tactic of adding just a little bit of falsehood to Truth, so be observant and discerning. It is a huge responsibility to ensure that ALL of what you are teaching is sound.

Consider two metaphors: In a relay race, when handing the baton to the next runner the giver must have good grasp of the baton and make sure the handoff is accurate and solidly placed in the hand of the next runner. In football, the quarterback must have solid footing when handing off the football to the running back, or the transfer may not take place or incomplete which could cause a fumble. The *giver* must have a good grasp on the item being transferred, and make sure the transfer to the *taker* is correct and solid. A school, and more specifically the teacher, must have a good solid footing in biblical doctrine to accurately transfer the item (lessons, information, curriculum, policies) to their students complete. Items transferred are incomplete without biblical connotation.

To re-iterate, *I believe the Bible's sound doctrine can be a part of every subject taught in a Christian school or Christian home school.* I would therefore challenge each teacher to choose their class curriculum based on sound biblical doctrine; to search out, and find biblical passages and references that support the subject matter being taught and use those passages in class. Include God's Word in everything that is taught; it takes a little extra effort, but the rewards are immense.

The hand off of your subject to your students needs to come from a solid biblical foundation.

- ***Sound doctrine* means healthy.** Eating nutritious foods produces a healthy body. A healthy body is better able to produce good works for the Lord. Truth produces a healthy spiritual wellbeing. Biblical Truth is the foundation of proper thought, wisdom, attitudes, and actions.

The New Living Translation has verse 1 as "promote the kind of living that reflects *wholesome teaching."* Please make sure you staff members act, talk, teach, and live as a reflection of sound biblical doctrine; sort of a mirror image of the Bible. (By words and example) And, teach your students to likewise live that way. Please make sure your teaching is *wholesome*, which is a word that means conducive to, or promoting good health, physical, and moral well-being. That is great advice for a Christian teacher!

Eating spoiled or rotten food can make you sick, and when sick, you are not very useful. The same goes for what is taught to students. Therefore make sure sound, healthy, and wholesome doctrine is only what is taught, so the learner can be useful (especially to God). Healthy Sound Christian schools teach a diet of Biblical Truth as the foundation of proper thought, wisdom, attitudes, and actions.

- ***Sound Doctrine* must be adhered to.** 2 Timothy 4:16 says "Take heed to yourself and to the doctrine. Continue in them, for in doing this you will save both yourself and those who hear you." Watch your doctrine closely! Make sure you teach what you know yourself to be sound doctrine! Don't waver from, or compromise sound doctrine! Those should be three sticky note reminders to all Christian school and home school teachers. Do that now, write each one on a note and put it in a place you will see it often. That is what Paul would say to Timothy today instead of "Take heed".

You must adhere to sound doctrine when you incorporate scripture into the teaching of your subjects. Always ask and then verify if what you are saying about the Bible and its application to your discussion is correctly interpreted and not out of context.

Is what you are saying about the Bible really what the Bible says. Paul continues telling Timothy why: you will save both yourself and the students who hear you. Let me put this plain and blunt: False or incorrect doctrine, even doctrine that is not wholly correct, is wholly wrong. And God calls that "destructive" and those that teach it are false teachers and their judgment is not idle and their destruction does not slumber in 2 Peter chapter), and in verse 17 calls them "wells without water, clouds carried by a tempest, for whom is reserved the blackness of darkness forever."

Pretty scary isn't it!? God takes adhering to and teaching sound doctrine seriously, and so should you, for your sake, and for the sake of your students. My advice is to not shy away from incorporating God's Word into your subjects, don't shy away even out of fear of getting it wrong, but be diligent to do so with prayer, verification of God's Word, and help from the Holy Spirit, which He will do, it is part of what Jesus said He would do in John 14.

- ***Sound Doctrine* means the Bible is sufficient as the basis of teaching.** The word doctrine means teachings. Make sure you are teaching sound *teachings.*

You see, the Word of God is God-breathed, and is profitable (valuable) for doctrine (teaching), for reproof (discovering and affixing blame), for correction (discipline to change behavior), for instruction (training) in righteousness, that the man (person) of God may be perfected, thoroughly equipped for every good work. (2 Timothy 3:16-17) This passage of Paul, inspired by the Holy Spirit, can be taken and used as individual elements, or it can be taken as this 7-step progression:

A godly person (the goal for you and your students) is perfected when the Bible is:

1) Understood to be *inspired* by God. Paul quite possibly invented a word here to explain this: the word in Greek

is *theopneustos*, and means *God-breathed*. It is not used anywhere else in the Bible. The meaning of the word is pivotal to Christian life. It means the whole Bible is breathed out by God. Sometimes God gave exact words to the writers to use, other times He used their thoughts, experiences, or inspired them what to write. That means when the Bible is read, God is speaking. It means you can trust the whole Bible.

2) Considered very valuable, useable, profitable, or serviceable.
3) Taught as the foundation for Christian living.
4) Used for pointing out error. Error in doctrine, thought, or behavior.
5) Used to correct that error. (And, to not repeat that error)
6) Used for training how to live the right way. Righteous living is the goal.
7) So that people (you and your students) may be perfected and thoroughly ready for anything they do (every good work).

John 1:1 and 1:14 establishes that the Word of God is Jesus. That is a very important concept to ponder, understand, and convey to students. So is the point that the volume or total amount of the Word of God is written about Jesus (as Hebrews 10:7 says). Studying and teaching God's Word and about Jesus is essential so that you and your students' mind is strengthened: "that their hearts may be encouraged, . . . and attaining to all riches of the full assurance of understanding, to the knowledge of the mystery (Truths) of God, both of the Father and of <u>Christ, in whom are hidden all the treasures of wisdom and knowledge."</u> (Colossians 2:2-3)

In Acts 20, Paul was teaching to the Ephesians, and said in verses 19-20 that he served the Lord humbly, with many tears and trials (it was hard and he had successes and failures teaching the Word of God) and that he kept back nothing that was helpful, but proclaimed to them and taught them publicly and from house to house, no matter who was the audience. In verses 27-30 Paul did not shy from teaching the Word of God. He was bold to declare to them the whole counsel of God, because the elders, pastors, and teachers were to shepherd God's people (including students) because they were purchased with Jesus' blood. Consider what Paul says there and apply it to your teaching of students. Paul says boldly teaching them sound doctrine is important because some people will come upon them like savage wolves, speaking wrong and distorted things to draw them away from the Truths in God's Word.

Paul goes on in verse 32 to say the Word of God is able "to build you up". Sound doctrine will build your students up, and give them a solid foundation to stand on; will give strength and confidence when treacherous times and people come. (And, you can bet they will come). In the Colossians passage just mentioned, Paul said that in Jesus are hidden all treasures of wisdom and knowledge; then he went on to say in verse 4 "lest anyone should deceive you with persuasive words." To prepare for that deception, and to combat it when it comes, Paul said in verse 7 we are to be "rooted *and built up in Him*, and established in the faith, as you have been taught, abounding in it with thanksgiving."

The Word of God, Jesus, is what we are to be made of. Yes, *made of.* That is why Paul used the words "rooted and built up". These are growth and construction terms. Please, if you are a teacher, make absolutely sure you are teaching correct *growth* and *construction* at your Christian school or home school. If so, your school and students will be sound.

Qualities of Teachers (from verse 2):

"Teach the older men to be temperate, worthy of respect, self-controlled, and sound in faith, in love and in endurance."

Your school's Administration, Teachers, Coaches, and Staff are to maintain certain qualities. As mentioned earlier, Teachers are to be true biblical Christians. This portion of the passage has specific qualities that I am sure God wants teachers to have. We will look at each one individually:

They are to be temperate.

> TEMPERATE: Marked by moderation: as a**:** keeping or held within limits**:** not extreme or excessive**:** mild b**:** moderate in indulgence of appetite or desire c**:** moderate in the use of alcoholic beverages d**:** marked by an absence or avoidance of extravagance, violence, or extreme partisanship. (Merriam-Webster)[20]

That is a great definition, it gives me an idea of a person that is *middle of the road, even keeled*, or *has it all together.* A person should not be excessively flamboyant, *a loose cannon*, or *unpredictable or erratic*, because Jesus wasn't. If you are a school administrator, you should ask yourself "how does each of our staff members measure up to that definition?" Remember, we want people to see Jesus *in* us, more than they see us. Be honorable and dignified, sensible, and spiritually healthy.

Worthy of respect.

> RESPECT: A person held in high or special regard **:** esteem**:** the quality or state of being Esteemed. (Merriam-Webster)[21]

2 Peter 3:14 tells us to "give diligence that you may be found in peace, without spot and blameless in the sight of people." Philippians 2:14 says "Do all things without complaining and disputing that you may become blameless and harmless, children of God, without fault in the midst of a crooked and perverse generation, among whom you shine as lights in the world, holding fast to the Word of life"

Teachers, have as your state of mind that you want your students to respect you; to want them to be like you in their heart. This is an incredible responsibility because your words and actions need to be worthy of their respect. How do you do that? Paul says by holding fast to the Word of Life!

Self-controlled.

> SELF-CONTROLLED: Restraint exercised over one's own impulses, emotions, or desires. (Merriam-Webster)[22]

Remember we Christians are to let our mind control our emotions, not visa-versa. 1 Peter 1:13 tells us to "Therefore gird up the loins of your mind." Here is how we do this:

1) Pray often. Doing so helps you focus on God.
2) Be careful what you think. (Biblical thoughts) (Phil. 4:8)
3) Be self-controlled, don't give way to wrong desires, and control your imagination.
4) Study the Bible *daily*, and then live what you learn from the Bible.
5) Watch where you put your hope. (If it disappoints you, it's the wrong hope)
6) Be determined to do what is right. (Col 3:23-24: whatever you do, do heartily as if to the Lord and not to men.)
7) Develop a hatred for sin.
8) Live here like a stranger. (Our home is in Heaven)
9) Love one another deeply, from your heart and mind. (Love intentionally)

Sound in faith.

We already covered that "sound" means free from problems or defect, and therefore "sound in faith" means Teachers (and all Christians) are to be free from problems with their Christianity.

They must be solid in their faith. They must have good biblical knowledge, be able to counsel students on biblical matters (or know when they should refer the student to someone that can better help the student, and know who that is), and they must know what it means to act like Christ. Above all, a Teacher should be sound enough in their faith that they teach as Jesus would have. By that, I mean with the attributes of Jesus such as humility, calmness, patience, with love, unselfishness, confidence, firmly, and with a servant mindset.

The Christ like attributes that teachers should have are very important. I have found, from my own observations of the teachers at the Christian school I am involved with, that the most effective teachers are those that are humble, unselfish, patient, and gladly serve their students; those that can sit down amongst the students and humbly teach on their level. Teachers like that not only teach a subject, but ensure each student has learned the subject before moving on. (And we all know different students learn differently) Those teachers also command the respect of the students, yet do so by still being close to them or communicating with them at their level.

Conversely, I have observed the less effective teachers are the most prideful teachers. They *lord it over* their students. For example, those teachers seem to be annoyed that their students aren't learning as fast as they should, or have little patience with them. Those teachers seem to have troubling issues about them such as the need to discipline more than usual, apathy among their students, receive criticism from students and parents, have lower class participation, and their students have lower grades. Now, I don't mean to equate spiritual maturity with the effectiveness of a teacher, but there can be a correlation worthy of pursuit. We also must be careful to equate the students' fondness of a teacher with the effectiveness of that teacher, but again, there *could* be a link there to consider. I do know some very effective and great teachers that are new Christians. I also know some great and effective teachers that are proud of their abilities and let you know them. But I know that strong, confident, humble, servant-like Teachers seem to be the most effective, and I also know that the Bible says pride is a sin…and Satan uses pride to harm Christian schooling.

A sound Christian school will have teachers that are endeavoring to be sound in faith, and teach as Jesus would have taught.

Sound in Love.

This one is huge! Pay attention to this quality of teachers, it is important, and takes a lot of effort. Do your teachers love to teach? Do they love the subject they teach? Here is a tough one: do they love their students? Here is an even tougher one: do their students love them? I am reminded of this line from a song: "They will know we are Christians by our love." Can that lyric be said about your schools teachers? Can it be said about you? Here is a saying that I really like, because I have found it to be so true: "Your students won't care how much you know until they know how much you care." Take that to heart. It takes effort to show love in the classroom, and it takes *extra* effort to show the same love to every student without partiality. Paul started out the love chapter in 1 Corinthians 13 by saying that without love, a person could be like sounding brass, or a clanging cymbal (just a bunch of noise). And then in the next sentence Paul said even though he may have lot of gifts such as understanding, knowledge, and faith, without love he was nothing. Then, he said that even with all his good deeds and sacrifices he made, they were worthless without love. So from that, I could stand on fairly firm ground saying that a teacher without love is nothing but a *worthless bunch of noise.*

The Bible commands us to love. In John 15:2 Jesus commands us to love one another. And in Matthew 22, a Lawyer asked Jesus about the greatest commandment and Jesus' answer to him (and us) was to love God with all your heart, soul, and mind, and then He quickly added that the second is like it, that you should love your neighbor as yourself. Teachers should model this love. Referring back to Paul's love chapter where he mentions the elements that make up love; I am sure you know them, but they need to ALL be part of teacher's love: Love is patient, kind and caring, not envious, not prideful or boastful, is not rude, not selfish, not provoked, does not seek revenge; does not rejoice in iniquity, but rejoices in the Truth; bears all things, believes all things, hopes all things, and endures all things. Love never fails. Teachers, please work on having all of those.

A sound Christian school will obey the commands of the Bible to love, and be characterized by all elements of love from 1 Corinthians 13.

During the annual graduation ceremony at our Christian school, nearly every graduating senior with opportunity to speak at the podium, mentions the very same thing: they thank a specific teacher. That particular teacher has made a positive impact on each student, and they say things like: "I want to thank "Mr. G" for helping me get through these last few years", "Thank you Mr. G for your help and guidance", "I want to thank Mr. G for just listening to me", "Mr. G, without you, I don't know how I would have made it." "Mr. G., you are a blessing to this school, and to me." So… does your school have a "Mr. G"? Do you have more than one? If you are a teacher, are you that type of person to your students?

The teenage years are rough for students, and getting rougher as the character and morality of our society dwindles, even in a Christian school, so are you helping them through with biblical based guidance? Are you someone they can come to in complete confidence and trust? Parents may be doing everything right in raising their teens, but a school still needs at least one "Mr. G". He loves the students and they know it. Mr. G. is a real person, and a real honor to Jesus whom he loves and serves in his job. He does not assess his effectiveness as a teacher or his love for students by whether they love him back or mention his name at graduation, but by his obedience to the Word of God.

A sound Christian school will have a "Mr. G." that students can confide in for biblical based guidance, support, or to just listen to them in confidence. "Mr. G" is effective because he honors and models the Word of God.

I really like Josh McDowell's comment "Rules without relationships results in rebellion." His insight is wonderful and in line with God's plan. Have you noticed the better our relationship is with God, the better we obey His rules? Remember, God wants a relationship with us so much, He sent His Son to pay the penalty for our sins so we can relate with Him. We parents and educators can certainly learn from those. As with 'Mr. G", in developing a relationship, it is important to *connect* with students. Relationships become the *vehicle* used to convey lessons, rules, and values.

One additional thought I would like to mention here is about teens again. One of the difficulties in being a teen is being accepted. Teens are going through the period in their life where they want to be independent, their own person, and to be accepted as a valued person. Teachers can tend to not recognize this, and fail to convey to the teen they have value. If you are a teacher of teens, please make an effort from your heart to make each teen feel valued. Also, teens hear a lot of rules, and get disciplined and corrected for breaking those rules, as they should. However, this should be done in a way that still lets them know they are important and have value, and is not demeaning to them. Then they need reassurance that their value as a person is not diminished, but through proper response to the situation, can be improved. One suggestion on how to do this, is to explain what the rule was that they broke and why the rule exists, why disciplinary action needs to occur, how the discipline will help them not break the rule again, and then after the discipline, reassure them that you have forgotten the offense, iterate your acceptance of them, and your confidence in them improving. Oh, and if appropriate, give them a hug.

A sound Christian school will instill value in their students, even during discipline.

Sound in Endurance.

> ENDURANCE: The ability to withstand hardship or adversity; especially: the ability to sustain a prolonged stressful effort or activity (Merriam-Webster)[23]

Endurance is a trait few have, and those that do have it, had to learn it. Endurance is *what comes out of the oven* when you mix learned discipline, determination, confidence, and some hope and trust in God and God's will. Teaching is a profession that requires endurance.

The writer of Hebrews tells Christians to have endurance in chapter 10 verses 35-36, and 12:1-2. These are great passages so please look them up and study them. Also remember Paul, when nearly done with his ministry, said in Second Timothy that with *endurance* he fought the good fight, kept the faith, and finished the race. What Christian school teachers do is tiring, has hardships and adversity, and can be a stressful effort. However, enduring is a noble endeavor if done with biblical love and focus. Keep up the fight, keep the faith, and finish the work as a teacher training young Disciples of Christ.

Teachers at a sound Christian school will recognize this biblical requirement of endurance, learn it, and work at gaining it. Then, will also find a way to teach it to their students.

Reputation of Teachers (from verses 7 & 8):

"In your teaching show integrity, seriousness and soundness of speech that cannot be condemned, so that those who oppose you may be ashamed because they have nothing bad to say about us." A person's reputation is of great value. It is valuable to the person, to God, and if the person is a Teacher, then great value to the Christian school. Paul tells in this passage why it is so valuable and the two ingredients needed to have a valued reputation: Integrity, and serious and sound speech.

Integrity.

> INTEGRITY: Firm adherence to a code of especially moral values. An unimpaired condition. The quality or state of being complete or undivided. (Merriam-Webster)[24]

Integrity includes honesty, incorruptibility, soundness, sincerity, righteousness, and completeness. Integrity comes from the word *integer*, as in a whole number, complete, not lacking anything. As a Christian, integrity is when Scripture, your heart, your words, and your deeds are all in harmony.

When you search the Bible for the word "integrity" you find it in these contexts:

- "Integrity of heart" 1 Kings 9:4
- "Job is still keeping hold of his integrity" Job 2:3
- "until I die, I will not retract my integrity" Job 27:5
- "judge me, O LORD, according to my righteousness, and according to my integrity in me." Psalm 7:8
- "You uphold me in my integrity, and set me before Your face forever" Psalm 41:12

- "The integrity of the upright shall guide them; but the crookedness of traitors shall destroy them." Proverbs 11:3
- "Better *is* the poor who walks in his integrity than he who *is* perverse in his lips, and is a fool." Proverbs 19:1
- "The just walks in his integrity; his sons *are* blessed after him." Proverbs 20:7

Several places in Scripture you will find the phrase "integrity of heart". The heart is where integrity starts, and is where integrity comes from. Proverbs 4:23 says "Guard your heart with all diligence, for out of it springs the issues of life." Ponder that passage for a while.

In our passage from Titus, Paul said "In your teaching show integrity."

The teaching at your Christian school should show integrity, honesty, incorruptibility, soundness, righteousness, and completeness.

When General H. Norman Schwarzkopf was asked what he thought was wrong with America, he responded with "a lack of integrity." One of the qualities of a sound school is to have integrity as teachers and staff, and to teach students to have integrity. Signs of a Teacher having integrity are:

- They have control of the situation and the classroom.
- They model Jesus in all they say and do.
- They model the fruits of the Spirit (love, joy, peace, patience, kindness, goodness, faithfulness, gentleness and self-control).
- Their fruits of the spirit are consistent, as well as consistent with their actions, values, methods, measures, principles, expectations, and outcome they expect.

Integrity is the opposite of hypocrisy. If successful, with God's help (and He *will* help, because integrity of the heart is so important to Him) Teachers, and by extension their school, will be a "light unto the world". Possibly even a remedy for what is wrong in our society, and in America.

"And this I pray, that your love may yet abound more and more in full knowledge and all discernment, for you to distinguish the things that differ, that you may be sincere and without blame for the day of Christ, being filled with fruits of righteousness through Jesus Christ, to the glory and praise of God." (Philippians 1: 9-11)

Serious and sound speech

> SERIOUS: Requiring much thought or work, of or relating to a matter of importance, not joking or trifling: being in earnest, excessive or impressive in quality, quantity, extent, or degree. (Merriam-Webster)[25]

As mentioned in Chapter 3, *sound* means free from flaw or error…based on thorough knowledge and experience…valid and having true premises…showing good judgment or sense.

Jesus said in Matthew 12:34 that "out of the abundance of the heart, the mouth speaks." So, in our Titus 2 passage, Paul listed integrity prior to good speech for a reason: It is sequential. Therefore make sure your speech, what you say and write:

1) Comes from much thought (which takes some time and some work).
2) Is impressive in quality.
3) Comes from sound doctrine (biblical knowledge and experience).
4) Is legally and logically valid, true, and agreeable with scripture showing good judgment or sense.

5) From a Christ filled heart. It is evident if so, and evident if not.

Ephesians 4:31 says: "Let all bitterness, wrath, anger, clamor, and evil speaking be put away from you will all malice." Do whatever it takes, even drastic measures if necessary, to get rid of those detrimental things mentioned so they do not affect your speech, attitude, and testimony. Hebrews 13:7 says students are to consider and emulate the outcome of the conduct of their Teachers. So make sure actions and conduct is worthy to be copied!

Colossians 3:16-17 says we are to "let the word of Christ dwell in us richly in all wisdom, teaching, and admonishing one another." Wow! That is one serious verse for teachers! Here is another one: "Let your speech always be with grace, seasoned with salt, that you may know how you ought to answer each one." (Colossians 4:6) Salt purifies, preserves, and ads flavor, a great metaphor of how Teachers should talk.

In addition to being the right thing to do, verse 8 of Titus 2 says our serious and sound speech should be such that those who oppose us may be ashamed because they have nothing bad to say about us. What a wonderful aspiration for Christian schools! – that your speech is such that no one can say anything bad about you.

The speech of teachers (as well as staff and Board members) in a sound Christian school should silence those that oppose Christianity and the Bible, and to make the gospel of Christ believable.

Qualities and Reputation of Your Students (from verses 9 & 10):

This next section of the Titus 2 scripture, in the light of Qualities of Sound Christian Education, refers to the requirements of students:

"Teach bondservants to be subject to their masters in everything, to try to please them, not to talk back to them, and not to steal from them, but to show that they can be fully trusted, so that in every way they will make the teaching about God our Savior attractive."

To be bondservants.

A "bondservant" is a person that has chosen to willingly serve a master. Some bondservants served their master without pay, but relied completely that the master they served would take care of their needs. It is a term that means true and whole hearted devotion to serving the master they love. Paul opened many of his letters saying he was a bondservant of Jesus Christ. In this Titus passage, it refers to those serving the church, and can also be taken to refer to employees, and to students.

The application here is twofold: First, a sound Christian school should teach and require that students are to simply respect, and be wholeheartedly devoted to Jesus Christ. Second, that a sound Christian school should teach and require students to respect, and be wholeheartedly devoted to their teachers, coaches, and others in authority at the school. Remember those that are in authority, such as teachers and administrators, are placed there by God's will (Romans 13:1), and students should understand that biblical principle. When students learn to respect the authority God has placed there, they will willingly be devoted to them and to obey them as well. Hebrews 13:17 is very important for students, so please teach this verse to them: "Have confidence in your leaders and submit to their authority, because they keep watch over you as those who must give an account. Do this so that their work will be a joy, not a burden, for that would be of no benefit to you." (NIV)

To be subject (obedient) to.

Obedience to teachers and administrators is a requirement of students in a sound Christian school. In life, obedience to authority, including parents, supervisors, police, and government officials, is a requirement of a Christian and is part of a Christian witness, no matter the circumstances (unless the Christian is required to disobey God). It also means to respect them, and to honor them. Hebrews 13:17 says "Obey those who rule over you, and be submissive, for they watch out for your souls, as those who must give account. Let them do so with joy and not with grief, for that would be unprofitable for you." This passage tells students three things:

1) Obey teachers and those in authority, and be submissive to them because they have your best interest in mind. The phrase *watch out for your souls* comes from the military term of the soldier whose responsibility is to guard the camp and keep out any intruders or enemies so the others can give all their attention to their tasks.
2) Teachers and those in authority must give an account. Their responsibility is to their boss, and to God. So students should trust them and what they are doing.
3) Don't grieve Teachers or those in authority, so they can fulfill their duties with joy. Students should not be bothersome to them, shouldn't be unruly, a pain, or cause trouble. Students should be good, obedient, and compliant, because if they are, Teachers and those in authority will be joyful and the learning experience in school will be joyful for students as well. When the environment is joyful a student learns more, which as the passage indicates, is most *profitable* for them.

In everything you do.

As mentioned above, students need these qualities for life. A sound Christian school understands they *train for life,* not just for the next test. This also means in all of their daily life, not just in front of a teacher or someone in authority (when home, when with friends, when alone). My Father used to tell me "Your true character comes out when no one is looking." That applies to outward actions, as well as thoughts. Students' thoughts should not differ from their actions in front of someone in authority. Students should endeavor to control their thoughts and their imagination. Most sins start in a person's imagination. Teach them to say no to certain thoughts. Philippians 4:8 is very helpful to do that: "Whatever is pure, lovely, of good report. . .think on these things."

To try to please them.

Students should give their best efforts to please their school teachers and administrators. This goes hand in hand with obedience. Students are to appreciate and emulate their godly teachers (so make sure you are godly Teachers!): Hebrews 13:7 says to "Remember your leaders, who spoke the word of God to you. Consider the outcome of their way of life and imitate their faith." (NIV)

To not talk back.

This also goes hand in hand with obedience and being well pleasing. Talking back insinuates defiance, disobedience, lack of respect, lack of trust, disloyalty, selfishness or pride, and poor character. It includes complaining, grumbling, or murmuring, which God hates (remember the Israelites in the wilderness?) All of these are not becoming of a believing Christian, and damages their gospel witness. Teachers and administrators that tolerate students' talking back are fostering those sinful traits in the student, and encouraging that student down a path of their own destruction, and is detrimental to furthering the gospel of Christ.

To not steal.

Some versions of the Bible say "pilfering", some say "embezzling". For employees, stealing includes outright theft, working less than you are paid to work (less than 60 minutes for an hour of pay), and giving less than 100% of your effort. For students, it means to not cheat, because cheating is stealing, and stealing is a sin. Additionally, as Paul says in 2 Timothy 2:15, students should give all of their efforts to school work, and studying: "Be diligent to present yourself approved to God, a worker who does not need to be ashamed, rightly dividing the word of truth." This means students should give 100% of their efforts in school, less than that is stealing. Similarly, doing *just enough to get by* is not being diligent, not trying to be approved to God, and is stealing.

To show they can be fully trusted.

Fully trusted means to show fidelity, to show full loyalty, and to have full devotion. Being trusted is a wonderful trait of a believing Christian. Sound Christian schools should teach students to be honorable, and trustworthy, and students should endeavor to attain trustworthiness.

To make the teaching about God our Savior attractive.

The lives of students attending a Sound Christian school will make people want the Gospel of Christ! I love the way the King James Version says this: "that they may adorn the doctrine of God our savior in all things." The qualities of a sound Christian school (sound doctrine – God's Truth – salvation for sinners) should adorn the students like beautiful attractive attire, or like the beauty and attractiveness of a flower.

Teachable spirit.

One more quality that students at a sound Christian school should have is a *teachable spirit*. Jesus mentions in Matthew 18:4 that we are all to have a humble and teachable spirit as children do. Children should love to learn, even when they are a teenager (and portray they think they know everything) they still love to learn. Develop a healthy love for the Word of God in your students, so that they love to learn how the Bible relates to all of the subjects they are taught.

Teachers and administrators, if you picture each of your students in your mind, can you say that each one is adorned with the doctrine of God? If not, then there may be a lack of *quality* in the soundness of your Christian school. May I ask that you teachers, administrators, and board members to take that thought, relate it to when students receive their graduation diploma, and adopt a famous advertising slogan from Zenith: "Quality goes in before the name goes on."

In Other Words… (from verses 11 to 15):

"For the grace of God that brings salvation has appeared to all men. It teaches us to say "No" to ungodliness and worldly passions, and to live self-controlled, upright and godly lives in this present age, while we wait for the blessed hope—the glorious appearing of our great God and Savior, Jesus Christ, who gave himself for us to redeem us from all wickedness and to purify for himself a people that are his very own, eager to do what is good. These, then, are the things you should teach. Encourage and rebuke with all authority. Do not let anyone despise you."

Paul ends this passage to Titus with a review. Sort of an "in other words..." paragraph where Paul makes the following key points:

- The grace of God has allowed salvation to come to all who believe
- Because of God's graciousness through Jesus, we should honor Him by:
- Saying "no" to ungodliness and worldliness.
- Living self-controlled lives.
- Living upright and godly lives in our age today.
- Waiting for, and focusing on, the blessed hope, which is when Jesus returns.
- Remember Jesus gave Himself for us to redeem us from all wickedness.
- Jesus purified us for Himself.
- Since we belong to Jesus, we are to be eager to do what is good.
- Make sure Jesus is *Lord* of our life.

Salvation transforms lives, and through the knowledge of God's Word and the help of the Holy Spirit, true Christians *want* to do good. Some un-saved person once said "Show me your redeemed life, and I will then believe in your redeemer". Make sure your lives show you are redeemed. Make sure your lives show Jesus is *Lord.*

Those all are the things Christian schools are to teach their students, as well as encourage or require from teachers, staff, and administration. School teachers and leaders are also to rebuke students if they do not do those things, and are to do so with all authority because those things all come from the Word of God. Notice these three sequential verbs in the Titus 2 passage: *Teach...encourage... rebuke.* Do you see the pattern there to follow? John MacArthur uses similar words in his commentary on this verse: "These three verbs identify the need for proclamation, application, and correction by the Word."6 Please, please don't forget to encourage. Students are in school to be taught, and teachers are to rebuke when appropriate, but students also desperately need encouragement, it is an essential component of the three.

We are to hold fast to these things from the Word of God, and to not let anyone despise you for doing so. Do not allow any rebellion against Gods Truth either.

While teaching on this Titus 2 passage at our Christian school board meeting one evening, a staff member asked "Isn't a student allowed to have free will?" Absolutely! Free will, or choice, is paramount to Christianity. We are, however talking about schooling. (Teaching and training.) We are to train a child to make right choices. We are to train a student's heart. Give them a moral compass to help them make correct choices, a compass where the needle points to Jesus Christ, the author of morality. In other words, with free will, comes responsibility, and responsibility is based on a set of morals, values, or code of ethics. We are to teach our students that Jesus Christ is the author of that moral code of ethics, and His Word is the authority they are to be responsible to.

I want to accentuate that last sentence with this element: **A sound Christian schools priority is the training of the students' HEART, and understands that "heart work is hard work", and is diligent to that endeavor.**

Responsibility of Teachers (from James 3:1):

This may be a good place to bring up the grand caveat of teaching...the prestigious admonition...the big forewarning...that verse which should be on the mind of all teachers: "My brethren, let not many of you become teachers, knowing that we shall receive a stricter judgment." (James 3:1)

This passage is not to discourage teachers, but to warn them of the seriousness of teaching *sound doctrine*. It is my opinion though, if the judgment will be stricter on teachers, then conversely the rewards will be greater for those that pass the judgment positively.

James goes on in the subsequent verses in the passage to say that words spoken are very important and must be of sound quality. This reminds me of the line in the movie Spiderman, where Peter's Uncle says to him "With great power, comes great responsibility". Just as the power Peter had when he became Spiderman, Teachers also have great power: The power to train and shape minds and lives. That is a HUGE responsibility that teachers will be held accountable to parents, and to God, for the quality and soundness of their teaching.

This aforementioned power is given to teachers by God. This passage also comes to mind, and seems to apply here: "But we have this treasure in earthen vessels that the excellence of the power may be of God and not of us." (2 Corinthians 4:7) Teachers have a responsibility to God to be correct in their teaching, and to use any and all tools necessary to do the job. So just as a good mechanic has the proper tools to work on cars correctly and knows how to accurately use those tools, God can give Teachers the tools to teach, if they learn them and how to use them.

Sound Christian schools employ teachers that enthusiastically gain and use the tools required to teach effectively.

God does not require perfection, but He does require us to try our absolute best to attain it. Teachers should pray for perfection in biblical accuracy and Truth in the subjects they teach. Then, teachers should give all due effort to research, learning, and application of the biblical Truth. If you are a Teacher doing those, God will honor your desire and efforts for Truth and relaying it to your students in *every* subject you teach.

In a wonderful Christian movie called "Time Changer", (a Rich Christiano film, which I highly recommend) one of my favorite lines is where the main character played by D. David Morin is speaking to a class of high schoolers and says "If science and the Bible disagree, then science is wrong." That may be a controversial statement to some, but the premise should be paramount in the thinking of Christian school teachers. Teachers should ask "what does the Bible say about ________", and set out to find the answer. If you are a teacher and do that, I think you will be surprised at what you find. God's Word is awesome; let Him speak to you and your students through it.

In John chapter 17 Jesus prayed for all of us believers. I would encourage all teachers to read His prayer and see what part of that prayer you can actively do in the lives of your students. Notice in verse 17 where Jesus prayed to the Father: "Sanctify them by Your truth. Your word is truth." Jesus said right there what Truth is! Teachers, you should endeavor to be an obedient servant of God as He works through you to sanctify students with God's Truth.

Sound Christian school teachers endeavor to give 100% of effort to attain biblical accurate Truth, and to relate that Truth effectively to their students in all scholastic subjects.

Chapter 8

Lessons From Ezra

After the last long chapter, here is one short and to the point. There was a Scribe in Old Testament times named Ezra who studied the Law of Moses (the first 5 books in our Bible). He studied them so well, it has been said he could write them down from memory! Ezra came from the lineage of Aaron with the qualifications of a priest. He took his job very seriously since a Scribe was expected to answer questions people had about the Law of God and explain it in an understandable way. Ezra was a wonderful teacher, and must have thought the best way to teach something is to learn it to the point of *memorizing* it.

Here is my favorite passage from Ezra: "…the good hand of his God was upon him. For Ezra had prepared his heart to seek the Law of the Lord, and to do it, and to teach statutes and ordinances in Israel." (Ezra 7:9-10)

This wonderful description is perfect for teachers, and Christians in general. There is a pattern there requiring self-discipline and maturity, which should also be taught to students. It goes like this: Ezra prepared his heart (cleaned out any sin or preoccupied thinking, and made sure his attitude was that of humility and openness to God), and probably prayed, then studied God's Word, and then applied God's Word to what he was doing, then he taught that to others. He studied and practiced God's laws in his own life before teaching it to others. This is a common sense *recipe* for successful teachers. It is a recipe that must be followed in order for Christian teachers to be obedient and used by God. Here are the ingredients of this recipe, which MUST be done in order:

- Prepare our heart
- Pray
- Seek God's Word
- Do God's Word
- Teach God's Word

The Persian King Artaxerxes (the pagan ruler of the world) was so impressed with Ezra's knowledge of the Bible in that day, and his teaching, that he let Ezra and the captive Israelites free to return to Jerusalem. He even authorized and set up funding for them to rebuild the Temple of the Lord and for offerings to the Lord! Oh do I pray that our Christian schools have teachers like Ezra!

There is another lesson for us later in chapter 7 where Ezra gives credit where credit is due, not himself or the King, but he praises and thanks God: "Blessed be the LORD God of our fathers, who has put such a thing as this in the king's heart, to beautify the house of the LORD which is in Jerusalem, and has extended mercy to me before the king and his counselors, and before all the king's mighty princes. So I was encouraged, as the hand of the LORD my God *was* upon me; and I gathered leading men of Israel to go up with me." (Ezra 7:27-28)

There is one more lesson from Ezra applicable to Christian school and home school teachers in the next chapter: "…that we might humble ourselves before our God, to seek from Him the right way for us and our little ones and our possessions." -Ezra 8:21 Here we see another pattern or recipe to follow:

- Humble ourselves before God. (God resists the proud, but gives grace to the humble.)
- Seek from Him the right way: (Prayer and Bible study together is how to seek Him)
- For us
- For our children or students
- For our possessions

Seeking the right way from God simply will not happen if we are not humble. We must prepare our heart before we pray and read His Word, and that means making sure we have the proper attitude. Humility before God means no pride in us at all and only focusing on God and His purposes, not on ourselves. That puts us exactly in the proper posture for Him to speak to us through His Word so we can wisely discern what the right way is for us and our children/ students. I like how Ezra also included seeking God's guidance for the proper use of the possessions He has blessed them with for His glory.

Ezra was a teacher devoted to prayer, studying God's Word, living what His Word says, successfully teaching it to others, and praising and thanking God. He was a firm teacher and leader, responsible, obedient, and courageous, rebuking and correcting the people when needed, yet he remained humble. A person used greatly by God.

Sadly, other godly people in the Old Testament started out seeking God and obeying Him, but that seemed to fizzle out. Most of the kings of Israel were that way and 2 Chronicles 12: 14 tells why as a commentary to the decline of King Rehoboam who was David's grandson: "And he did evil, because he did not prepare his heart to seek the LORD."

Later, in chapter 15:12-15 the people realized the trend, and took action. "Then they entered into a covenant to seek the LORD God of their fathers with all their heart and with all their soul; and whoever would not seek the LORD God of Israel was to be put to death, whether small or great, whether man or woman. Then they took an oath before the LORD with a loud voice, with shouting and trumpets and rams' horns. And all Judah rejoiced at the oath, for they had sworn with all their heart and sought Him with all their soul; and He was found by them, and the LORD gave them rest all around." Did you notice the penalty they had for not seeking God? Wow, that should tell us how important it is to seek Him and His will not only for our own life, but for our teaching, and our administration at Christian or home schools. I also like how at the end of that passage God gave them "rest all around" when they did. That indicates to me being determined to set our heart to seek God, and obey Him, will usually bring peace and a good night's sleep.

Chapter 9

Sound Leadership

Having worked at a few businesses over the years, including 25 years at the same company which I eventually became a majority owner and General Manager, I have really noticed there is a certain style or personality each company seems to have. That style and personality very closely resembles that of the leadership or person in charge. Having also been involved in Christian schooling for about 15 years, I can say that remains true there also; the style and personality of a Christian school closely resembles the leadership of the school.

Style and Personality

The soundness of your school is directly related to the identity of the school. That is, what people *perceive* about your school. So I want you to think about what your school's style and personality is like. If you were to poll several parents, asking them to describe the style and personality of the school, what would the answers be? Maybe you should actually conduct that poll, and do it every several years or so. A sound Christian school *knows* exactly what their style and personality is. They also know what their style and personality *should* be, as a goal for their school, and purposefully works to attain that goal.

What are the style and personality traits of a sound Christian school? As mentioned above, they are patterned after the leadership of the school. The Administrator, Head Master, Principal, whatever your school leader is called, that is who to focus on here. (For this book, I will use the term Administrator) If your school has a Board of Directors, or Trustees, their style and personality is also applicable here as well, but quite often those folks are not directly involved in the daily managerial duties of running the school, so are not as influential as the Administrator, the topic of focus here.

The leadership of the school is twofold. Yes, two distinctly different leaders. You need to realize this, and you need these two leaders to be both in charge, and congruent. The two leaders are Jesus Christ, and your schools Administrator. Notice I used the word "congruent", which means "in agreement, corresponding to or consistent with each other or with something else" (Encarta Dictionary). Consistent agreement between the Administrator and with Jesus Christ is imperative, and consistent agreement "with something else" is with God's Word, and the style and personality of Jesus. So grab a hold of that concept firmly; which again is that your leadership style and personality, also the style and personality of your school, is consistent with the style and personality of Jesus Christ.

"He is married to the school!"

There is a biblical analogy or pattern for the Administrator and school to emulate: Marriage and the family. I know that may raise an eyebrow and I may stretch this to try to make if fit into schooling, but let me explain my thinking here, and see if you agree with me or not. Marriage is the union of a man and a woman. They are equal people, yet have different roles and duties, and both have input toward decisions in the marriage and family, but the man is set up by God as the leader and has final say. When those different roles and duties are understood, appreciated, and allowed to flourish, that union works perfectly. Now, keep that in mind and think of the parallels of these:

- Jesus Christ and his Bride, the Church.
- A Man, and his Bride the Woman.
- A Christian school Administrator, and the school staff.

Now don't snicker, and please do NOT go off on any tangents that do not belong here. Just focus on the roles and duties of each partner, and the parallels of the biblical requirements of marriage. Let me set the groundwork with Ephesians 5:22-33: "Wives, submit to your own husbands, as to the Lord. For the husband is head of the wife, as also Christ is head of the church; and He is the Savior of the body. Therefore, just as the church is subject to Christ, so let the wives be to their own husbands in everything. Husbands, love your wives, just as Christ also loved the church and gave Himself for her, that He might sanctify and cleanse her with the washing of water by the word, that He might present her to Himself a glorious church, not having spot or wrinkle or any such thing, but that she should be holy and without blemish. So husbands ought to love their own wives as their own bodies; he who loves his wife loves himself. For no one ever hated his own flesh, but nourishes and cherishes it, just as the Lord does the church. For we are members of His body, of His flesh and of His bones. "FOR THIS REASON A MAN SHALL LEAVE HIS FATHER AND MOTHER AND BE JOINED TO HIS WIFE, AND THE TWO SHALL BECOME ONE FLESH." This is a great mystery, but I speak concerning Christ and the church. Nevertheless let each one of you in particular so love his own wife as himself, and let the wife see that she respects her husband."

Just as God is the head of Jesus Christ, Jesus Christ is the head of the church, and so likewise the husband is the head of his wife and family. Jesus loved the church so much, He was obedient to God, and gave Himself for her. He sacrificially and humbly gave all he had for her. That is what the husband is to do for his wife also. I am suggesting also the school Administrator for the staff.

Reading further in the Ephesians passage, husbands are to love their wives as they love themselves. This means putting the interests and well-being of their wife at least as more important than their own. He should make it his goal and aim in life to love her, to serve her, and to ensure she flourishes. The school Administrator is to similarly do so: love (as in brotherly love), serve, and to ensure they flourish.

Just as Jesus is the leader of the church, the husband is the leader of the marriage/family, and he has authority and final say on things. The husband requests and requires her input, and honors her input, but he has the final say on decisions, since his role is the leader. He is not demeaning to her or ridicule her, (not to her face, nor to others when she is not around) he does not treat her as "second class", but as an equal. He honors her and the unique abilities she brings to the marriage, and gives her roles to do commensurate with her abilities. He does not "lord it over her", but encourages her and supports her, he removes obstacles that prevent her from flourishing, he teaches her to be better with love and tenderness, he has compassion for her weaknesses, and encourages her strengths. He places her on a high pedestal.

She is to submit to his authority and honor and respect him. She is to lovingly encourage him to be a great leader, to support him, and to back him up. She is not to degrade him nor criticize him, (to his face, or to others when he is not around) but to support him. She is to encourage him to be the unique man God has made and is making, and she recognizes that may be different than the man she wants him to be. She follows the pattern of marriage where God says she and he are equal in standing, but they have distinct differences, and different roles, duties and responsibilities. (I won't get off topic with examples). And one of her roles is to be the follower and supporter, not leader.

Because of the God-given differences of a man and woman in marriage, the husband and wife complement each other to make a perfect union, in fact they are better together, than individually (the Bible uses the term "shall become one"). When those differences are understood, and encouraged to flourish, and roles and duties are performed according to these differences, the marriage works awesomely. You might say as like a well-tuned automobile. And when the automobile runs well, the designer and creator are honored and praised; likewise God is honored and praised when marriage runs well.

In a school, the Administrator and staff complement each other, and when differences are understood, and duties assigned accordingly, similar to a marriage, when that pattern God set up is followed, the school is better for it, and they act as if they are one. Maybe like one well-tuned automobile, and as above, honor and praise are due for the designer and creator.

Schools are not parents

I cannot quit this topic without adding a little bit about the roles of children to parents from Ephesians 6, and to draw from that passage a correlation of students to Administrator and staff. I will develop this further in a subsequent chapter, but to make the point now in brief: just as children are to obey, and honor their parents, students are to obey and honor their Teachers and Administrator. God has only a little bit of instruction to children in the Bible, but what He does give is simple, to the point, and demanding. It is found in a few places in the Bible, but Ephesians 6:1-3 is real good: "Children, obey your parents in the Lord, for this is right. "HONOR YOUR FATHER AND MOTHER," which is the first commandment with promise: "THAT IT MAY BE WELL WITH YOU AND YOU MAY LIVE LONG ON THE EARTH."" (Emphasis added)

Children are to obey and honor their parents in the Lord. How children obey and honor God is shown in how they obey and honor their parents. Can you understand that requisite? Parents are to be obedient to God in the training of the children God has entrusted to them, and their accountability for doing so is to God. In the same way, Children are to be obedient to their parents, and their accountability for doing so is to their parents.

When Parents entrust their children to a Christian school, they should not be saying they are turning over their responsibility to God for the training of their children to the school, they should be saying they have prayerfully and discernibly made the decision that the school will help them raise their children as they believe God requires them to. To go along side of them or assist them in raising and training their children biblically so they may impact the world for Jesus. That includes rules of conduct and discipline, so parents should fully understand the rules and policies of the school, as well as the disciplinary actions the school takes when those rules are broken. Therefore, school administration and staff need to make sure children understand the equal importance of obeying the school as with obeying their parents.

A sound Christian school goes along side parents in training their children to impact the world for Jesus. Obedience and discipline are equally important in the home and at school.

The godly requirements aforementioned are why our enemy, Satan, is engaged in an all-out attack on marriage and the family. The function and responsibilities of the family to each other and to God is Gods pattern that works perfectly when followed correctly, which glorifies Him. So Satan wants to ridicule it, subvert it, de-emphasize it, and tear it down. He wants to say it is antiquated and not needed any longer, or that marriage and/or family can be something different than what God's perfect plan for it is. You can see in our headlines how Satan is doing on in our society today. That is why a sound Christian school upholds, promotes, and honors the biblical requirements of marriage between one man and one woman, the roles and structure God has of that marriage, and upholds, promotes, and honors the biblical requirements of children.

A sound Christian school's Administrator and staff promotes and upholds Gods perfect plan of marriage and family structure.

Be like Jesus

Back to the style and personality the school Administrator is to have. Specifically, the Administrator should be like Jesus. Let's think about what Jesus is like. What words come to mind? What traits does Jesus have? I will mention some here, but you may have others also that I didn't write down here. I am sure yours will be just as good to make my point as the ones I come up with. All accurate descriptions of Jesus will be what the school Administrator should be like. Here are a few I came up with:

Loving. The first word I think of when describing Jesus is love. John 15:12-13 describes this love, and is Jesus that said it: "This is my commandment, that you love one another as I have loved you. Greater love has no one than this, that someone lay down his life for his friends." A school Administrator should be loving, which includes caring, devoted, and warm.

Sacrificial. Reading the passage above, you will also see that Jesus loved people so much, that he willingly and sacrificially gave His life for them (us) so they would not have to pay the penalty for their sins. That is the ultimate sacrifice and display of love. Since few of us will show our love for others by dying for them, the best way to show love is some sort of sacrifice. A school Administrator is sacrificial, and gives up his/her time, things he/she pridefully holds on to, gives up some worldly or material things. Defends God's Word, even when it hurts. Defends his/her staff even if it hurts.

Humble. Jesus was God's Son in Heaven, ruler of the universe. He was obedient to God the Father, and became a human, without a home or place to lay his head, and ultimately was executed to save people. That is humility. Yet, He made such an impact as a leader that He changed the whole world. A school Administrator is to be humble, obedient to God, not a powerful ruler but a servant. Humility is a trait of a true Christian, even Christian leaders, because they endeavor to be like Jesus.

Serving. Jesus served God, and served people. He met people's needs wherever He went, especially their need for salvation from their sins. A school Administrator is to serve his school and serve his staff. Yes, SERVE them. My favorite book on leadership is "Management: a Biblical Approach" by Myron Rush. In it, Mr. Rush states that "The authoritarian approach to management stimulates discontent, frustration, and negative attitudes toward leadership"[26] "...the biblical approach to management can be defined as follows: Management is meeting the needs of people as they work at accomplishing their jobs."[27] He also quotes Lee Brase, a Christian leader who said "I have discovered that if you train a man, he will become what you are, but if you *serve* him, the sky is the limit as to what he can become".[28]

Disciplinarian. This includes the words "just", "firm", "impartial", "equal", and "loving". A school Administrator knows and holds to the rules of the school, and the rules of the Bible. He/she is not biased, treats all staff the same, treats all students the same, showing no favoritism. When discipline is required, the Administrator patiently and methodically researches all facts to ensure the truth of the offense, determines appropriate punishment, explains the offence - especially from the biblical point of view – including the sin committed and requests/requires repentance, administers the punishment, then assures their love for the offender, and forgets the offence. Just as God does.

Hard worker. Just as a good servant works hard for their master, the school Administrator works hard as if working for the Lord.

(Ephesians 6:7: "with goodwill doing service, as to the Lord, and not to men,") Jesus worked hard; VERY hard. The Administrator's good hard work ethic is to be the example and standard for his/her staff to follow. Just as he/she is to follow the example and standard set by Jesus.

Encourager. One of my favorite people in the Bible, one that I suggest we all try to emulate, especially the school Administrator, is Barnabas (his name was actually Joses, but people called him Barnabas which means "encourager"). In Acts 4:36-37 Barnabas was a land owner that sold his land and gave the money to the apostles, which was quite an encouragement at that point in the early church. In Acts 9:27 shortly after the conversion of Saul (Paul) when Saul went to Jerusalem to try to meet with Jesus' disciples, they all were afraid of him and didn't believe him, except for Barnabas, who broke away and stood by Saul's side and explained to them about how Jesus met Saul on the road and how Saul preached boldly in Damascus.

When Paul didn't want Mark to go with him on another missionary journey, Barnabas saw that Mark felt dejected, and took Mark back to his home town and spent time encouraging him. This was such a great help to Mark that he wrote the Gospel of Mark, and was later reconciled with Paul. Barnabas had an uncanny way about him that saw good and God's purpose in people, and tried to bring that out.

Also in Acts 11:19-26 when the growth of the early church was sputtering, Barnabas went out into the surrounding areas "...and he exhorted them all to remain faithful to the Lord with steadfast purpose, for he was a good man, full of the Holy Spirit and of faith. And a great many people were added to the Lord." He stayed in Antioch for a little while, and it was there that the disciples were first called Christians. Barnabas was part of the first "Christians", a nice tie-in with the term *Christian school.* Administrator, be like Barnabas, see the good in people that God has given them, and encourage them with that. Encourage your staff and students "to remain faithful to the Lord with steadfast purpose". Be a person that is "a good man, full of the Holy Spirit and of faith" (they are different). I would like to add that you cannot be an "encourager" if you are selfish, and prideful. Both of those are sinful traits, and are NOT traits of Jesus. So be others-centered, and a Christ follower.

Obviously this list of traits can go on for a while, but let me mention a few more, and I want you to read each one, and ponder them, and if you are a school Administrator, ask if you have these traits. If not, what are you going to do to gain them?

Patient. Honorable. Courageous. Passionate.
Joyful. Self-controlled.

Biblical Requirements of the School Administrator

At a Christian school, the Administrator is like a Pastor, as well as a General Manager of a business. Not one or the other, but both. Since a Christian school means the school emulates or follows Christ, then I think the biblical requirements for Pastors should apply to the school Administrator. While a Christian school board member, I used the following criteria when interviewing potential candidates for our Administrator opening, and actually used the same criteria when considering new fellow school board members. The criteria are primarily from Paul's letter to Timothy:

> "The saying is trustworthy: If anyone aspires to the office of overseer, he desires a noble task. Therefore an overseer must be above reproach, the husband of one wife, sober-minded, self-controlled, respectable, hospitable, able to teach, not a drunkard, not violent but gentle, not quarrelsome, not a lover of money. He must manage his own household well, with all dignity keeping his children submissive, for if someone does not know how to manage his own household, how will he care for God's church? He must not be a recent convert,

> or he may become puffed up with conceit and fall into the condemnation of the devil. Moreover, he must be well thought of by outsiders, so that he may not fall into disgrace, into a snare of the devil." 1 Timothy 3:1-7 (ESV)

According to this passage, we can use these requirements for an "overseer" which we can also call the position of school Administrator or Board of Directors member. Let's look at them individually: (Please note this passage uses male gender specific language, and I will in kind, however, feel free to change the gender terms if your Administrator applicant is a female, they all apply basically the same)

Noble task. The leadership of the school is a noble endeavor. The person's heart must fully be *into it.* Training precious children is one of the noblest tasks of humanity. Parents have been given by God the responsibility to train and school their children biblically. When those parents entrust a portion of that training to you, the leader of the school, they believe in your noble ability to fulfill that responsibility.

Overseer is used to describe a person in charge. The Greek term is used for a Bishop, Pastor, or other responsible leadership person. It is a term used to describe persons that lead, labor in the Word or Doctrine, and teach (5:17) to help the spiritually weak (1 Thess. 5:12-14), and care for the people they lead (1 Peter 5:1-2).

Desire. There are two different Greek words used here. The first means *to reach out after.* It describes an external action. The second means *a strong passion* and refers to an inward desire. This describes a person that outwardly pursues the duties because of a strong inward desire.

Must is a particle stressing emphatically (that a blameless life is required).

Be above reproach (blameless) in a criminal sense, there can be no accusation of wrongdoing that can be made against him.

No overt or flagrant sin can mar his life, and the reputation of the school. He must be an example to be followed. (A personal background check might be wise)

Husband of one wife. Literally a *one woman man.* The Greek term describes a moral and sexual purity. This requirement is near the top of the list because it is the area most leaders are prone to fail. This does not mean the person must be married, after all it was written by Paul, who was single.

Temperate. This can also mean *alert, watchful, vigilant,* or *clear headed.* The person must be able to think clearly. I like to use the term "being infinitely aware of your surroundings." Know what is going on, be aware of the *scuttlebutt* that is muttered amongst others. The person must command the respect of others, so that there is no need for others to mutter about him/her behind their back. The person must be known as James said in chapter 5 verse 12: "But let your "Yes" be "Yes," and your "No," "No"."

Self-controlled. This is a well-disciplined person that also knows how to organize his priorities, orderly, and also is serious about his duties as well as spiritual matters. Self-controlled can also mean confident. A leader that portrays firm confidence is one that is respected and looked up to. A school Administrator is a self-controlled and confident leader whose "yes" means yes, and whose "no" means no. (A biblical requirement of every Christian)

Respectable. The person must have, and be aware of the respect of those under him, as well as parents and students. He must also have respect for his boss: the School Board. And, of course, respect for God and God's requirements.

Hospitable. This word comes from the compound Greek word meaning *love of strangers.* As with all spiritual virtues, he must set the example; his life and livelihood must show his spiritual character. (Romans 12:13, Hebrews 13:2, and 1 Peter 4:9 are good passages to consider here)

Able to teach. This is, after all, what a school is about. 2 Timothy 2:24 says to "not quarrel but be gentle to all, able to teach, patient, in humility correcting those in opposition, … so that they may know the truth." This more applies to a church Pastor, but in a school setting, it still does similarly in that the Administrator must have at least some qualities of a teacher, particularly relating to teaching from God's Word where bringing up a scripture passage and relating it to a situation that has come up. It can also be applied to the school Administrator being able to teach some of the classes, but not necessarily.

There are basically two types of General Managers of a business: The first is able to perform all the tasks in the company. They can fill in when an employee is sick, and they can teach each position to a new employee. This is important in a leader because it enables them to be respected by their employees. The other type is able to delegate tasks to those best suited to doing them. This manager is good because he can recognize the strengths and weaknesses in employees, and place people where their strengths will flourish. He can suggest training for the employee, if it will be beneficial, to enhance their weaknesses toward a strength. Both of these manager types should be able to remove the obstacles that prevent their employees from performing to their utmost abilities. This certainly applies to the administrator of a school.

Not given to drunkenness. Obviously you do not want drunkard.

Not violent but gentle. He must react to difficult situations with calmness, control, and gentleness. (2 Tim 2:24 again) You should not stand for any violence.

Not quarrelsome. Peaceful, reluctant to fight, one who does not promote disunity, or disharmony. Not contentious. Not one to stir up trouble.

Not a lover of money. Not covetous (one of the 10 commandments). The Administrator must be motivated by the love of God and His people, not money. He must have a full understanding and maturity that God will meet his needs, and that God will give him the desires of his heart (Ecclesiastes 5:18-20).

If he is working for money, it reveals a heart set on the world, not things of God (Matt 6:24; 1 John 2:15). Granted, he needs to make enough money to afford to live and function in the location. Paul says covetous characteristics is a trait of false teachers (Titus 1:11 and others).

Must manage his own family well. For if a man does not know how to rule his own spouse, children, and finances well, how can he take care his school, co-workers, students, and the budget? There must be a good and long pattern of solid family leadership in biblical principles, moral issues, discipline, finances, taxes, laws, etc. His children must respect him with reverence and submission.

Must not be a recent convert. First, he must be saved, his testimony must be sincere and according to Scriptures: there must be a specific time of realization of his depravity, true repentance, acceptance of Jesus Christ as his redeemer, and a commitment to follow in Him.

A new believer has not had sufficient time in the Word as well as the Word vs. the world to be an effective Administrator in the situations that come up daily. A mature Christian will not be as tainted by the world's sin as a recent convert would. A mature Christian should be well grounded in the Word so as to be discerning and to view any situation in the light of the Scriptures. He will also understand how to glorify God, enhance His kingdom, that "all who desire to live godly in Christ Jesus will suffer persecution." (2 Tim 3:12)

Not puffed up with pride. A new Christian would be tempted with pride in this leadership role. Pride is the first sin, and it has been said that all sins have pride as their root. Pride is what caused the fall of Satan. Pride denies the work of the Lord. Humility is a trait of Jesus, and a goal of His followers.

A good reputation. A good testimony in the unbelieving community. How can he make a spiritual impact on those who do not respect him? (Matt 5:48; Phil. 2:15) The person must be known for what they are FOR, more than what they are against. 2 Timothy

2:15 says "Be diligent to present yourself approved to God, a worker who does not need to be ashamed, rightly dividing the word of truth." The reputation of the school depends on the reputation of the Administrator.

Not fall into disgrace and the snare of the devil. The warning of attacks and snares of the devil is mentioned twice in this passage. Paul (and the Holy Spirit who helped him write this) knew that the leader of a church or school is the prime target of the enemy Satan. If Satan can get to the Administrator of the school in any way, the Christian school would be disgraced, and God's reputation would be harmed. That is precisely what Satan wants, godly endeavors to not succeed, be harmed, or be disgraced, and the best way to do that is through the Administrator. I have seen several Christian school Administrators be dismissed due to issues where the devil has gained a foothold. Paul mentions pride because that is usually where the Administrator is vulnerable. Make sure this does not happen to your school. However, I predict it will unless you and your Administrator are aware it can happen to even the most godly and spiritually minded people because even they still have a sin nature, and Satan knows how to use that for his purpose of hurting a Christian school. I suggest this become a topic of discussion periodically between the school Administrator, and the Board of Directors (or other leadership) to identify any issues, weaknesses, or potential problems that are or could arise, and to do so openly, humbly, lovingly, and biblically. "Accountability coffee" is something I suggest where the Board and Administrator meet informally for prayer and open discussion about any vulnerable personal or professional areas the enemy can attack, and to ensure and encourage spiritual growth.

In a very similar passage to 1 Timothy 3 reviewed in detail above, Paul also writes these similar requirements to Titus where in chapter 1 he mentions a few additional things. In verse 9, he requires leaders (of a Christian school in our parallel here) to hold "fast the faithful Word according to doctrine, that he may be able, by sound doctrine, both to exhort and to convict…" Biblical knowledge and the willingness to turn to the Word of God in teaching, and discipline are paramount in a Christian school. He goes on in verses 10-16 to warn that there are many people who say they know God (say they are Christians), but in their works, they actually deny Him. Their actions don't match their statements, and that disqualifies them for the position. Read that passage during your evaluation process and do your *homework* and check references, because these people will say what you want to hear to get the job.

In Titus 3: 1-2, Paul also helps Christian schools choose an Administrator when they inquire of their applicant what his or her thoughts and actions are concerning the rulers and authorities over the Administrator position. In this passage, Paul requires the Administrator to be subject to, and obedient to, the rulers and authorities of the school. These rulers can be the school board or trustees, church leaders, parent's group, as well as to God. Romans 13:1-2 also affirms the Tutus 3 passage that submission to God (and His Word) demands submission to the authorities God has placed, and how a person handles those in authority reveals their Christian character and testimony, as well as ramifications if not compliant. I have seen Christian school Administrators terminated because they developed a wrongful (sinful) view of those over them forgetting that God has chosen and placed them there: "Let every soul be subject to the governing authorities. For there is no authority except from God, and the authorities that exist are appointed by God. Therefore whoever resists the authority resists the ordinance of God, and those who resist will bring judgment on themselves."

The applicant for position of Administrator is to be ready for every good and godly work, and is not to speak evil of anyone, not quarrelsome, but is patient and meek. In Titus 3: 9-11, Paul says to avoid applicants that are divisive, contentious, engage in foolish disputes, because he says such things are unprofitable and useless. He even says what should be done with a person like this: "Reject a divisive man after the first and second admonition, knowing that such a person is warped and sinning, being self-condemned." So not only are you to steer clear of such people as applicants for Christian school leadership, but use these principles during periodic reviews of the leader to ensure they are maintained. If a person you have now in leadership does not measure up to these principles, you should consider discussing the deficiency with the leader, remediation, and/or possibly even letting them go, and find a suitable replacement.

A sound Christian school follows God's requirements for their Administrator or leadership, and keeps them accountable to those requirements, even if dismissal and a replacement is necessary.

Chapter 10

Philosophies, Beliefs, and Academic Areas

As I write this, my Wife and I are beginning the process of choosing a Christian college for our daughter to attend. She was not interested at first, but is now starting to warm up to the idea. Teens seem to not do a whole lot of thinking about the distant future, even though she is in the 11th grade, and college decisions are not too distant. That is one of the reasons parents should still be heavily involved in nurturing their teen.

The internet is a wonderful thing in this regard because you can visit the web site of any college or university and get a real understanding of what is important at that college, albeit a polished "spic and span" view, but nonetheless, great information. Not only can you view the academic offerings, you can see extracurricular activities, financial information, and great photos and even videos of the college. One of the first things I do is check out the "Statement of Faith" (or similar term) of the college. This is their theological beliefs in a concise form. All should have a statement of some sort where their beliefs, those they deem important, are stated. It is very clear to me that all schools have spent a lot of time working on this statement, and I applaud that.

Statement of Faith or Beliefs

Just as Christian colleges, and most churches, Christian grade schools should also have a readily accessible "Statement of Faith" on the school web site, bulletin board, and/or school policy manual handed out to enrollees and their parents. What should it contain? That is up to you to decide because it is *your* statement. Coming up with your own is a process that you must go through. It involves prayer, Bible study, and seeking biblical counsel. The process of developing your statement will define your school, and your school will be defined by your statement. It should contain the core biblical doctrines you hold dear, and are not willing to waiver from. Once you have it, I ask that you refer to it often, post it in various places, make it accessible to anyone, memorize it and have it be on the tip of your tongue as Peter required of us in 1 Peter 3:15.

The Purpose you Propose to Purvey

Since the "Statement of Faith" is unique to your school, but with certain unwavering biblical doctrines, there is also a philosophy that you adhere to. Sort of a *why we do what we do and how we do it* statement. Although not as imperative as your statement of faith, it is a great thing to have in written form why you do what you do: "The purpose you propose to purvey".

Your "Statement of Purpose", "Mission Statement", or "School Philosophy" should have several issues covered. Adherence to Gods Word is paramount and at the forefront. To equip students for Gods purpose is also important. Philippians 4:8 comes to mind when I think of this. Your Christian school should be concentrating on things that are true, noble, just, pure, lovely, of good report, virtuous, and praiseworthy. How you do that in a teaching/academic environment is entirely up to you. It may be a challenge, but is certainly part of a sound Christian school. Your goal is to *turn out* students with that mindset, as well as students that bear the fruits of the spirit as found in Galatians 5:22-23.

A sound Christian school has spent the time to develop, refine, and publicly declare the core doctrines, beliefs, and values that define their school.

Yes, I said define. Those foundation biblical elements that your school stands on, and does not waver or compromise. The statement that you frequently refer to in moments of attacks or conflict, decision making or policy changes, hiring or dismissal of staff, acceptance or dismissal of students, and of course, discipline.

I would suggest that a school philosophy be based on, or include at least these elements:

Biblical basis. As mentioned previously, your school should equip students with a biblical world view. Specific biblical examples should be taught, and this book has many for you to incorporate. As a springboard, I would suggest you use 2 Timothy 3:16-17 "All Scripture is given by inspiration of God, and is profitable for doctrine, for reproof, for correction, for instruction in righteousness, that the man of God may be complete, thoroughly equipped for every good work."

Spiritual growth. A goal for students from your Christian school should not only to be true Christians, but be growing and maturing spiritually. Each semester or year you have a student, they should be more spiritually grounded and knowledgeable than the previous. Remember, one of the main traits of a true and growing Christian, is fruit. Do you see any fruit? Students may not have as much fruit as more mature believers, but there still should be some. Review Matthew 7, John 15, and Galatians 5:22.

Your students should be able to share their faith with others. They should have a biblical based moral compass, and have biblical based views on their home life, society issues, and even government issues.

Academic growth: Students from your Christian school should excel academically. We all know that scholastic achievement scores prove that on average Christian based home schooling or Christian schooling results in scores superior to those from the public government schools. Please ensure this continues. Competent well rounded academically sound students should be the result of biblical based schooling, and spiritual growth. "God doesn't turn out junk" is a simple, but profound saying. If your school is doing its job correctly, your students will shine academically.

Life growth. Some may call this cultural growth, I like to call it life growth. I always like to take a step back and look at the whole picture. Make sure students are well rounded. I have heard the phrase that if you study all the time, you will be a dull person. Extracurricular activities and sports are a MUST for well roundedness. Those activities teach things like teamwork, respect, rules, etc. that scholastic academics don't. Life application endeavors are also a MUST. An example is chemistry class has an accompanying lab. What you learn in the classroom must be practiced in the real world or application situations. You cannot learn much about welding if you never strike an arc. You cannot learn about evangelism if you never have the opportunity to evangelize. A student will not have an opportunity to be well rounded if one area is emphasized to the detriment of others. An example I have seen is too much homework given so the student does not have time for sports or even Church youth group activities.

One more suggestion is community involvement. The best and most memorable events of my life have been while volunteering. For a Christian school to be involved helping the community, is putting shoes on your Christian walk, and opens up tremendous doors for the spreading of the Gospel. You may consider having volunteer hours required for each school year or semester. This probably is age appropriate (older students), but does not have to be. You may even have a letter grade associated with the quality or effort of the volunteer activity, but volunteerism may not be school supervised which would make a letter grade impossible. The object here is that requiring volunteerism is a good biblical lesson and mindset for the student to learn and apply to their whole life.

The Best Student and the Best Schooling

Can you think of who was the best student in all of history?

Probably not a whole lot of surprise here, Jesus was the best student ever. His teacher(s) most likely were also some of the best ever, because of Philippians 1:6, which says that if God begins a good work, or has plans for you, He will complete that good work. God will provide all means and resources to accomplish His plans, and that includes good and godly Christian teachers for the students He has plans for. (He sure had plans for Jesus!) So I would assume Jesus' teacher(s) were the best ever. He was probably home schooled (hooray for home school!), but we don't know for sure. So, can you see part of the purpose of sound Christian schooling is as the vehicle through which God's will is completed in people?

There is not a lot of information in the Bible about Jesus' schooling or His childhood, but there is enough for us to learn and apply to Christian schooling. In Luke chapter 2, Doctor Luke (remember, Luke was a medical doctor as a vocation when He met Jesus) tells us in verse 40 that Jesus as a "Child grew and became strong in spirit, filled with wisdom; and the grace of God was upon Him."

I state elsewhere in this book that I believe wisdom comes from knowledge. Knowledge comes from the Word of God, and with that knowledge and wisdom come strength and confidence in the Holy Spirit to accomplish God's plans. A very basic lesson and purpose right there for Christian schooling!

Jesus must have been taught very thoroughly the scriptures they had in that day. He quoted a lot of scripture passages throughout His ministry in applicable context. Wisdom comes from understanding the knowledge learned, and in knowing how to apply the correct understanding of the knowledge learned, so He must have been taught how to use that knowledge. He had learned so well that when he was only twelve years old, he spent a long time (Luke says three days) during and just after the Feast of the Passover "in the temple, sitting in the midst of the teachers, both listening to them and asking them questions. And all who heard Him were astonished at His understanding and answers."

Now a question that is often raised has to do with whether or not Jesus had Divine nature here at this age or not. I don't think it matters. I think since we Christians are to be like Jesus, Christian schools and home schools can look to how Jesus was as a student, and endeavor to emulate Him and His schooling. In Luke 2:52, there is a little bit about Jesus as a student, and a LOT can be learned about Him and the quality of His education in this one verse: "And Jesus increased in wisdom and stature, and in favor with God and men." There are four areas of life that the schooling of Jesus addresses here: mental, physical, spiritual, and social. Sound Christian schooling must train children in these four areas, giving appropriate effort to all, and none at the expense of another. They are individual areas, but work together, and it takes all four to have a sound Christian student. Let's look at each of them:

- **Mental** I would assume this is your main focus in schooling. It is listed first for a reason. It is the foundation from which the other three build from, and the other three must have this to be of value. Mental includes academics or the knowledge of things, and the wisdom of how to use or apply those things. Mental must also include the knowledge of what is right and true. Mental must also include discernment, which means the thought process to evaluate and come to a conclusion on any topic or issue, usually based on the knowledge of right and truth. Mental means to think logically. Mental must also include self-discipline, which is the ability and maturity to control your thoughts and ideas, since everything begins in the mind as a thought or idea. Self-discipline is a mental ability for all areas of our life. Mental must include the understanding of a biblical world view, including the battle of good versus evil (God and Satan) as described in the Bible. It also includes the sinful nature of all people, the penalty for sin, that the penalty for sins was paid for by Jesus, and the purpose of life to serve Jesus as your Lord and glorify God, if you choose to repent of your sins and accept Him. Mental must include the tools necessary to serve God, and to recognize, resist, and possibly battle Gods enemy, Satan, as described in Ephesians 6:10-20. God said in Hosea 4:6 that His people were being destroyed because of their lack of knowledge, God wishes we become mentally great, which includes academics, and knowledge of Him and His laws.

- **Physical** We are not purely mental, but physical as well; they go hand in hand. A physically strong, healthy, and active person is a mentally strong, healthy, and active person as well. Teaching physical topics includes our bodies as the temple of God, and the proper use for our bodies, as well as some misuse topics (what is acceptable, and unacceptable to God). It also includes physical activity. Why do we have recess for children, gym class, intramural sports, individual, and team sports? I believe Jesus was strong and physically fit, and worked hard at the proper times to maintain it. I am a big proponent for sports in school, and sports teams for home schooled students to join. God created us to be physical beings, to use and enjoy the use of our bodies in glorifying Him in physical activity, and to learn valuable lessons. Sports teaches self-discipline, character, respect for rules and authority, boundaries, respect for others, it teaches confidence, work ethic, communication, responsibility, unity, and many other lessons in life, including winning and losing, and how to handle each. I praise God for sports because of it is a wonderful place to teach children the valuable lessons He wants them to learn. I would like to add a comment here that sports can also be an area where we can easily succumb to worldly views, instead of godly requirements. We are to portray the character of Jesus, not selfish prideful character that can be demeaning of others. Our coaches need to teach this. We need to be truthful. If a child makes a mistake, telling them "it's OK" is not the truth, but telling them where their mistake occurred, and encourage them to try again to improve is. Everyone is made by God with different abilities and different levels of ability, but all can be a glory to God. There are winners and there are losers, but losers can be winners if they gave 100% of their effort. How the game is played is more important than winning. Compromising your values to win is a horrible life lesson to teach in sports. Teach Christian values, and sports is a great place to teach, practice, and perfect those values.

- **Spiritual** As mentioned in the mental area above, Christian schooling must teach the biblical world view. Spirituality is part of this, of course, and must include the teaching and understanding of God's Word, the Bible. Spiritual comes from the Latin *spiritus* which means breathing. Religious and spiritual are two different things. Religion is people's attempt to please God, spiritual is taking on the nature or the very essence of God, and becomes a necessary part of us like breathing. In 2 Timothy 3:16, the Bible says that all scripture is "God breathed". Therefore, the meaning of being spiritual is to have as our nature, or our very essence, the Word of God. We are to live the Bible. In addition to that, the Bible teaches that we are created by God to have a relationship with Him. A relationship with God is so important to Him, that He sent His Son to die on the cross to pay for our sins, so we can have a communicative relationship with God without the barrier of sin between us.

God loves to communicate with us (prayer, and reading His Word) as in personal devotions and personal prayer time. He loves for us to try to understand Him, and to be obedient to Him, which is spiritual. He wants us to be involved in our local church, and a ministry of some sort. Sound Christian schools teach their students to live the Bible, to obey God, and to have a communicative relationship with Him. Spiritual also means to have and disseminate a biblical world view. Spiritual means to glorify God in all we say and do.

- **Social** We are to have and maintain relationships. We are to have companionship and unity among fellow Christians. Relationships are extremely important for growth as a Christian, accountability as a Christian, and the spreading of the Gospel. To be social, we must have the learned ability to reason logically, and to communicate effectively through rhetoric. Being social means to be friendly, courteous, caring, loving, respectful, serving, compassionate, trustworthy, God honoring, and edifying. By nature, people are selfish, self-centered, and proud (sinful nature we all have), which are detrimental to relationships with others, and to our relationship to God. To be social, we must have well developed mental and spiritual areas (see above). Kids today are the most social kids in all of history, with e-mail, texting, cell phones, and social sites on the internet. So Christian schools have a much bigger reason to teach Christian social skills. Teach do's and don'ts of e-mailing, politeness, etiquette, and social rules and courtesy. To re-iterate: being social is a learned skill, and as mentioned above, education must include teaching logic and rhetoric. Christian schools must teach others-centered, Christ-like social skills based on biblical mental abilities, and spiritual abilities, with the awareness and overcoming of selfishness and pride. Christianity is intended by Jesus to be a group effort. To be out in the world's "battlefield", but to regroup, huddle up with other Christians around God's Word, recharge, then go back out. We are to assemble as believers, encourage each other, hold each other accountable, and ensure each other is living an obedient, fruitful life in Christ. Sound Christian schools encourage their students to interact with other Christians outside of school such as church youth groups and Bible studies. Then teach that the extension to that is also important whereas Jesus said we are to be lights in a dark world. Remember the song "This little light of mine"? we are not to hide our light under a bushel, but to let it shine outside of the church and school environment. Being social is important to God, and should be to our Christian schools as well.

When a school puts so much emphasis on studies and homework that sports suffer (physical), church activities and personal devotions are deleted (spiritual and social), and there is no time to go bowling or to the movies with friends or to family events (social), something is wrong. In that environment, students are not given the opportunity to fully be like Jesus Christ.

Kids are underdeveloped and struggle through the next chapter in their life when academics and homework take priority at the expense of the other three areas, and there are many casualties. For example, kids cannot make it in college away from home, even though their grades are exemplary, and most of you know some of these kids, you just (wrongfully) assumed other issues are to blame. Now there may be other issues, but this unbalanced education described is a major issue.

When sports takes priority in a school, and students lack the scholastic education to even get and hold a job outside of sports, the school forsakes the students. When a school is "run" by lazy students or whimpering parents who demand easy and worthless subjects and simple tests, our society suffers and the school is a failure. A balance of the above four areas needs to occur, and it needs to be evident, and explained well to students and parents.

Teachers, Board Members, and Administrators, take this to heart, learn, evaluate, determine, and implement these four areas. Emulate the schooling Jesus had in the four areas above, and your students will burst forth when they graduate excited, well rounded, Christ-like, and glorifying Him, not soured and incomplete.

Sound Christian schools will ensure well rounded teaching of their students in the areas of growth of *mental, physical, spiritual, and social.*

Every Christian should endeavor to be a "little Christ" (part of the meaning of the label "Christian" is to be a "little Christ"). Students who call themselves *Christians* should learn to be like Jesus Christ, and teachers should help them to be a *little Christ*. What are some characteristics of Jesus Christ? Well, let's keep in mind that Jesus Christ is both fully God and fully man, so his characteristics include: Love (John 15:13, John 13:1), Joy (Proverbs 15:13, John 15:11), Peace (Matt. 5:9, Col. 3:15, Phil. 4:7), Patience (Romans 12:12, James 1:3, 12), Kindness (Eph. 4:32), Goodness (Matt. 19:16), Faithfulness (Matt. 25:21, Heb. 11:1), Gentleness (Isaiah 40:11, 2 Tim. 2:24), and Self-control (1 Thess. 5:22). Teaching those attributes of Christ to your students is part of a sound Christian school.

In a Nutshell

So, in a nutshell, a sound Christian school will prepare their students with a good foundation of biblical Truth so they will be "good and faithful servants" of Jesus according to the individual plan God has for the individual student. To look more deeply at what is in that nutshell, let's spend some time looking at HOW a sound Christian school will prepare their students to live a life of discernment with wisdom, according to God's will or purpose, utilizing the gifts God gives them, being obedient and honoring to Him, able to defend their faith, and be able to explain and spread the Gospel, prepared for any spiritual battle, while serving Him in their career with the character of Jesus:

- **Living a life of discernment.** Proverbs chapters 1 through 4 are mostly about discernment and how to have it. Solomon (one of the wisest people ever to live – his wisdom was given to him by God) spent a lot of effort in his writings about discernment, how to attain it, and that it has to be learned. He says it comes from knowledge (biblical knowledge for biblical discernment), understanding, and the proper application of that knowledge, which is called wisdom, to make correct discerning decisions.
- **With wisdom.** As mentioned above, wisdom comes from knowledge, they are two different things. Proverbs tells us in numerous passages (mainly chapters 1 through 4) to get knowledge AND to get wisdom, in fact Proverbs 4:7 says it is the principle thing, therefore we are commanded to get it. We have to physically make an effort to grasp it, and it takes work to keep it. It takes practice, and the renewing of our mind daily with His Word. Yes, Solomon says it comes from God's Word, and the knowledge of God and knowing God. Knowledge, wisdom, understanding, and discernment are all tied to Gods Word. So the preparation of our kids for life, and a sound Christian school MUST include Gods Word as the basis and foundation for knowledge, understanding, wisdom, discernment. Even in academic subjects.
- **According to God's will or purpose.** 1 Corinthians 7:17 says, "Nevertheless, each person should live as a believer in whatever situation the Lord has assigned to them, just as God has called them" (NIV) I am convinced that God has

a plan and a purpose for every true believer. His purpose in situations that may come up throughout our day, and His purpose in our career or vocation. Serving God and having a ministry is not restricted to being a pastor or missionary, but includes every place He places us. That may include serving God as a missionary, but it also includes every other viable vocation such as a welder, truck driver, secretary, farmer, teacher, or homemaker. Christian schools are to train their kids to serve God, and to work as if working for God as their boss, in everything they do, and that includes their career or vocation. (Ephesians 6:5-9 is one of several passages on this)

- **Utilizing the "spiritual gift(s)" His Word says true Christians have been given**. Teach that this is a biblical Truth (see 1 Corinthians 12:4-7), and it is for the edification of other Christians. If we don't use the abilities God gave us to help the body of believers, we are depriving that body of believers of something special that God has for them. Teach that God intends us to be of use to him: We are to obey that calling and to use what He has invested in us.
- **Being obedient.** Jesus said that if you love Him, you will keep His commands.
- **Learning about God and growing in Him.** Colossians 1:9-12 is a brief sequence of progression of the growing Christian: We are to be "filled with the knowledge of His will in all wisdom and spiritual understanding;" We are then to "walk worthy of the Lord, fully pleasing Him, being fruitful in every good work and increasing in the knowledge of God."
- **Honoring to Him**. If you are a Christian, you have God's *trademark* on you. You are His. He owns you. Your life should be an example of what a true Christian is. Teach that. More on how kids honor Him is to follow.
- **Defenders of the faith.** A defender of the faith will be able to respond to the issues in our world that can be construed

as attacks on Christianity. These attacks occur while in the world or outside the church, as well as inside the church. Yes, I said *inside* the church, because I think Satan is at work in our churches as much, or more, than he is working outside of it. Prepare students to confidently defend their beliefs. The key word there is "confidently", and kids that are confident in their beliefs have come to that confidence through careful teaching in a way that is understandable, possibly leading kids to arrive at the decision you have **led** them to (because most people's solid beliefs are those they have discovered themselves). Confidence also comes from practice, and many Christian schools have debate teams, evangelization field trips, situation responses, apologetics class, etc. to give their kids practice defending their faith. More on this later.

- **Spreading the Gospel.** Similar to being a defender of the faith above, but on more of an offensive platform rather than defensive. Evangelize, witness, explain the Good News, these are terms of the same thing – to spread the Gospel. Every Christian should have a ready answer to the hope they have (1 Peter 3:15, 2 Corinthians 3:12), and be able to explain how to be saved. After all, that was Jesus' last request before He went up to Heaven (see Mark 16:15).
- **Prepared for the spiritual battles that will come.** Ephesians 6 from verse 10 on tells us how to prepare for the spiritual battles. One of the main points to understand, and to explain to students is that we are all born with a sin nature. We all have a tendency to not do what God wants. Also, I believe we all have a weakness in a certain area in our life, and the Enemy knows that weakness and will exploit it. He will use that weakness to break us down, cause us to stumble, or use us to cause others to stumble. When we are aware of these things, we are able to better recognize the

battles that ensue there, and to have a chance, with God's help to overcome them. (1 Corinthians 10:13)

- **Choosing a career to serve God.** As mentioned earlier, some people think that you can only serve God as a Pastor or Missionary, and that is just not so. God intends us to serve Him in all areas of life, and in whatever vocation He leads us to. Whether that actually is a pastor, or a welder, an architect, teacher, factory worker, nurse, or in front of a conveyor belt, or in front of a sink and washing machine, we are to do everything for the glory of the Lord. We are to **serve** Him in whatever job He has placed us. We are to be salt of the earth, (salt has no value if not mixed with something else), or light of the world (light is not light if it is not in amongst some darkness) as a method of reaching the lost and of bringing glory to God. Christians are to work in their career as if working for the Lord, and let others see the Lord in us.
- **The character of Jesus with strength and confidence.** All true Christians are to make every effort to be more and more like Jesus. To grow spiritually, and to bear fruit for Jesus. In Philippians 3, even Paul said he was still growing and learning, and when he wrote that, he had been a Christian serving God almost daily for over 30 years!

In the first chapter of the book of Joshua, when God was preparing him to take over for Moses, God told Joshua several times to "be strong and of good courage". Joshua 1:5-9 should be on a plaque on a wall in every Christian school.

To be an effective Christian, we must be strong and of good courage. To also be confident in what we know to be true, especially concerning Gods Truth. We must have enough biblical knowledge to know how to respond to virtually all issues that come our way, whether they are attacks, or opportunities to evangelize. Remember the analogy in the earlier chapter about recognizing attacks of the

Enemy where bank tellers recognize counterfeit money by studying real money? Similarly, if Christian schools (and all of us Christians) insist on studying the Bible intently and with purpose, then the fake gospels, counterfeit religions, or even suspect comments that come along will instantly be recognized. Then strong, confident, courageous persons can point them out, and warn others, or defend their position of Gods Truth.

We must make sure our students have a well-rounded knowledge of scholastic subjects to be confident and courageous in various endeavors. An effective Christian school prepares their students to be strong and of good courage, and to confidently stand up to errors and attacks. Strength and courage is something that many people have to work at. As mentioned previously, students can learn these from preparing and giving speeches, school debate events, and other presentations to gain practice, and gain confidence. One thing to remember, and to exhort students to remember, is that strength and confidence also comes from Jesus through the Holy Spirit. He will come along side of them, and hold them up, giving them words, thoughts, and courage at the appropriate time according to His will. In John 14 and 15, Jesus said he would give us a "helper", literally someone to help prop us up when we need, and that is the Holy Spirit.

Strong, courageous people are few and far between any more. My parents' generation seemed to have many more of that type of people than my generation, and now our kids' generation seems to have even less. We have become too self-centered, too attached to comfort, to lazy, too video game enthralled, too centered on self-gratification and entertainment, too afraid of effort, too afraid of confrontation, and too afraid to offend people. No one cares to want to make a difference or take a stand. Their "yes" has become "maybe", and their "no" has become "I dunno". Parents and Teachers...please fix that!

A sound Christian school will graduate students that are confident, strong, courageous, and godly people that will make a positive impact, and will take a stand for God when needed. A person, as Jesus said in Matthew 5, whose yes is yes, and no is no.

Chapter 11

Why, What, and How

During my term as a Board Member/Trustee at a Christian school where I live, I presented a devotional that took nearly a year's worth of board meetings to cover. That devotional was called "How to Teach Children to Have a Moral Compass." I may turn that into a book some day because what I learned as a father, and as a school board member was extremely valuable, and on the other hand, severely lacking in our society, including Christian parenting and Christian schooling. I first stated that children are not born with a moral compass; it has to be taught to them. Then I developed three key points which are teaching children WHY something is taught to them, WHAT the consequences are, and HOW to think through and make a decision. A sound Christian school uses these three points, and does on two fronts: *pre-emptive* teaching of students, and during discipline.

Why Something is Taught.

We all know that the best teachers not only teach a topic or subject, but they explain *why*:

Why a math formula or equation is needed, why in English class a sentence is constructed that way, why in chemistry class "you do not mix those two chemicals together", why do they need to know this or that. I did horrible in calculus class because I was never told why in life I needed to know how to find the area under a curve...

Teaching a topic or subject takes effort and planning, but it takes extra effort and hard work to explain *why* the student needs to learn that topic or subject. Do that extra effort. Additionally, for the school Administration, all rules need to have a *why* attached. That is a blanket statement, I know, but I have heard some Christian schools being called "legalistic" (in a negative connotation), and when I asked or looked into the reason, found the rules were not overwhelming or excessive, as I assumed, but were simply not explained why they exist. At risk of oversimplification, saying "don't touch that" to a child is OK when they are very little, but at some point, they will want to know why, or will find out themselves. You will then need to say "don't touch that, because it is hot and will burn you". And may I add that I have found that putting the rules – and reasons – in the student's handbook may not be good enough, you may have to have your homeroom teacher go over the rules and why they are in place verbally.

In life's decisions the student makes, we must explain why the choice should be made, why the child should not do this or that, why a behavior is inappropriate, etc. Life is filled with daily decisions, some trivial, some very important. Teaching a child to understand the reasons, and the consequences of those decisions is paramount to a moral compass. Since Jesus is the author of morality, (I encourage you to evaluate and comprehend that statement!) a sound Christian school will tie each *reason* and *consequence* to Him and His purpose. Biblical reasons should be part of each "why" you teach.

Teachers should teach application, not just implication. The Bible teaches doctrine and duty, sound teachings then how to apply those teachings to life. Teaching about a topic is one thing, implying a result or consequence is the next thing, but many teachers end the topic there; teaching how to apply that topic or issue is quite another. I know this does not pertain to every subject or topic, but to those it does, it takes a little more effort, creativity, and possibly student involvement to teach application of the topic. For example: teaching that a thermal unit is a measure of heat derived from an energy source is one thing, teaching how to arrive at the thermal units it takes to heat the classroom is the next thing, but helping the students arrive at how many thermal units it takes to heat the classroom using electricity, natural gas, or firewood, may result in a discovery of cost savings that could help the school or the student's home. Likewise, teaching the application of biblical passages in real life issues is just as important, and the responsibility of any teacher in a Christian school. That, in itself, sets apart the great teacher from the average.

What the Consequences Are

When we ask a child why they did something, we all have heard the standard answer "I dunno". Most children do not intentionally make decisions that have bad or negative consequences. They want to please, and they want to do what they think is best (I know people have a sinful nature . . . but work with me here). People, even young people, want to succeed and be good at things. However, when teaching why something is taught, and what the consequences are, there are two things working against you: selfishness, and short sightedness.

Selfishness is a sin, it is rooted in pride, and we all are born with it, and continue to have problems with it to some degree or another. I believe pride is the root of all sin because it is what caused the fall of Lucifer prior to the creation of the world and man (read the account of this in Isaiah 14:12-14 and count how many prideful statements Satan makes prior to his fall), and we all know the effect that had, and continues to have on creation and man. Only by Gods help, and our recognizing it, can we work to eliminate this sin. A sound Christian school recognizes the sin of selfishness/ pride, deals with it effectively, and teaches what the consequences of it are. Hebrews 12:11 is a great verse for a purpose for discipline:

"Now no chastening seems to be joyful for the present, but painful; nevertheless, afterward it yields the peaceable fruit of righteousness to those who have been trained by it."

Shortsightedness is the other thing that is working against you. A young person's brain does not fully develop the mental capacity to consider the consequences of a decision or action until they are in their 20's. Most children, even most teenagers, cannot think "down the road", or into the future. Their world is small. Their ability to think into the future is limited to a short time, and probably not even to the next day. But, forward thinking (another way of calling it), is something that can and has to be taught. Educators MUST take a step back and understand that, and then help the child, with patience and understanding, to develop the thought process of considering the implications of their decision or actions. Sort of an *if you do this, then this is what will happen* approach.

A Christian schooling cliché passage of Proverbs 22:6 is so appropriate here, especially when read simply and as originally written: "Train up a child in his way, And even when he is old he will not depart from it." "Train up" is the first word, and is an action verb. Training takes effort, continual time, and discipline. Its original Hebrew term also has connotations to our term *narrowly* which means focused on specifics. Since this verse can be a warning, it implies biblical based training is the doctrine and guideline to use by the context of the passage, and if you do not, and allow the child to have their (sinful by nature) way, the child will not depart from their ways even when they are old. The term "way" can be taken as a course of life. Couple that with the statement in 2 Timothy 3:16-17 "All Scripture is given by inspiration of God, and is profitable for doctrine, for reproof, for correction, for instruction in righteousness, that the man of God may be complete, thoroughly equipped for every good work.", and you have a sound reason and basis for teaching that actions have consequences, and for teaching discernment in how to make decisions.

How to Make Decisions

Here is where the rubber meets the road. If successful at the previous two points, then this final point is a little easier. If why something is done, and what the consequences of decisions are not understood, then it is harder to help the child make their own correct and discerning decisions.

Telling a child to do, or not to do something "because I said so" may teach that child to respect and obey authority, which they should, but does nothing to teach the child to have a moral compass – to make correct decisions on their own, especially when you are not around. It also does nothing to train the child to have godly character. A sound Christian school teaches their students to have correct and biblical character, and tells them why, so they can make correct choices on their own.

You see, God gave us the ability to choose. (I am going to simplify this topic in an effort to portray how I think it should be taught to students.) His ultimate purpose of the ability to choose is that we either choose to love and obey Him, or not. When He created Adam and Eve, he placed a tree in the middle of the garden where they lived, and told them not to eat from it. He gave them the ability to eat from it, but ordered them not to eat from it. It was up to them to obey or not. God did so because with a choice, he would know for sure that their choice was genuine and sincere from them, and not because of being forced to choose to. If *forced* to choose something, then it is not really a choice. If we choose to love and obey God, then it is a genuine, sincere, and honest choice, and not forced, and that REALLY pleases Him.

An analogy is that I KNOW my Wife loves me because she has a real choice to. She doesn't tell me she loves me because I force her to, which wouldn't be genuine love, she tells me she loves me because she really does, and lets me know it in different ways and sometimes when I am not even expecting her to. That is genuine love she has for me because it is her own choice.

Most decisions come after considering why, and what the consequences would probably be, and obedience to authority, especially God. How decisions are made is by progressing through a process to make the correct choice. That process includes discernment, and making a correct decision after carefully considering the options in the light of the Bible. Most decisions can begin or end with the simple question: "Does it please God, or does it please self." The focus of our thinking or purpose of the decision is either based on God's will, or selfish will. This thinking tells a lot of who you are, and of your spiritual maturity. School age children need to be taught to think biblically, since thinking selfishly is our nature. It is not what you think you are, but what you think: you are.

Sound Christian schools train students how to be discerning, to think things through, and use proper judgment, viewing everything through the "spectacles" of Scripture.

When our daughter was a sophomore at our Christian school, she began to make some bad choices. She knew scripture, she knew what God wanted and required, but she still chose to not obey His Word, or her parents. Several teachers at her school recognized this in her life, and skillfully endeavored to correct her actions and back up our parental discipline. We thank God for them, and thank God she attends a biblical Christian school. She knew what was right and wrong, but evidently did not connect her wrong behavior with the consequences that result. Due to her age, and resultant mental developmental growth, I think she may not have had the mental ability to make that connection. Nevertheless, it took a God-controlled consequence of a sinful act of hers before she was able to realize the connection of the two, and to repent and change.

Sound Christian schools teach that actions have consequences, including sinful actions. Christian staff recognizes sin in their students, and tactfully addresses the sin, and explains the consequences of it, as well as God's righteous judgment of sin.

Rules of Conduct

Have you ever heard any of these comments?:

"The Bible is just a bunch of rules..."
"This school has too many rules!"
"I want out of this house and on my own so I won't have any rules!"

To be an effective Christian that is serving, honoring, and bringing glory to God, there must be rules, and the rules must be obeyed. One sign of maturity is when a person understands that rules are for our protection, and they actually liberate us rather than enslave us. God loved us so much, that He set in stone rules to protect us.

God gave us rules of conduct because we need them. Schools need rules of conduct. Society needs rules of conduct. They serve as guardrails on the side of the road of life to keep us from harm, or harming others. So, here are some new comments:

"Rules are good for schools."
"Without rules: chaos rules."
"God's rules RULE!"
"Rules are best when they are Bible based."

As previously mentioned, when God created Adam and Eve, He set a fruit tree in the middle of the garden, and told them not to eat of it. He made a rule. He created people with the ability to choose, and a rule to test that ability. Ultimately that choice is to show our love for God through our obedience to Him. Rules serve several purposes, some for protection (for ourselves, and/or others), some for lessons to be learned, some as tests. Many are all three. God chose the tree probably not because the fruit itself would harm them if eaten, but to test their obedience and ultimately their love for him. He put the tree in the *middle* of the garden, not on the edge of it, so Adam and Eve would see the tree every day, and they would be forced to make a decision every day to obey Him, or not. (More on that later)

Rules that protect us, or protect others are just that: protection. God loves us and wants to keep us from harm. Parents set some rules for their children's safety, like "don't touch the stove". Schools have those types of rules also, and should explain WHY those rules are in place: what they are protecting the students from.

Rules that are for lessons are also part of God's plan, and from His love for us. These rules teach us how to treat each other in a loving way, such as "do unto others as you would have them do unto you". Some rules teach us to respect and obey authority, even if there is no reason for the rule other than that; military boot camp uses rules to teach this. Recruits are ordered to go out in a field and spend the day digging a hole, then the next day, they are ordered to fill the hole back in. The purpose is to obey and respect authority even if you don't understand why, or do not see a purpose in the requirement. Some rules teach self-discipline, a trait that has to be taught, because it does not come natural.

Some rules are to test what we have learned, or test our obedience. The tree in the Garden of Eden is a good example because obeying the rule to not eat of it was mostly a test to find out whether Adam or Eve loved (and therefore obeyed) themselves, or their God, and which of the two they trusted more.

Rules bring a "cause and effect", than that needs to be understood by everyone. Privileges come from being responsible and obedient; discipline comes from being irresponsible and disobedient. Just as this biblical premise is evident in scripture and reinforced by God, so Christian schooling should have and practice this concept. Following and enforcing those rules should have continuity and equality for all students (and staff), or the rules are not effective. Favoritism for some students, or letting some students "slide this time" sends the wrong message and undermines the reason of the rules. Enforce the rules the same way to all. A sound Christian school will have rules for protection, for learning, and for testing. The school will explain the reason for the rules and will enforce and re-enforce those rules equally for all.

"In our school, rules rule". Schools have a published handbook or policy manual that includes rules of conduct. A sound Christian school has two biblically based written rules of conduct, one for students, and one for staff/teachers. These are published and given to the respective recipients. They steer the person to honor and be like Jesus Christ, and I encourage you and your school to make sure each rule has a biblical reason why it is there, including its *cause and effect.* It should be the proper length or quantity of rules, as too few are ineffective, and too many results in a lack of respect for them. A saying of mine applies here: "Keep it simple, and keep it biblical".

A Christian school realizes that God put the primary responsibility of teaching His rules on the family home. (Deuteronomy 6:7) Therefore the Christian school should serve as an extension of the home in this regard, but should understand many homes, even Christian homes, falter at that responsibility. Therefore the Christian school should ensure they are in the position to pick up any deficiencies in Gods requirement, and ensure their rules are biblical and complete. It will be the result of much prayer and godly guidance. It will result from research, it will be Bible based, and the result of good biblical counsel. It will include applicable State and Federal laws, and be approved and maintained by the school's Board of Directors. It should also be reviewed by Pastors or other clergy as well as an Attorney (part of the counsel mentioned prior).

Once your schools rules are established, refrain from changes or modifications showing respect for the process that it resulted from. I also recommend parents or guardians be given a copy of the school's rules of the student, and asked to read them, and possibly even sign them as read and agreed to. This will hopefully reduce any contention, and provide a place of reference and refuge.

Always remember to tie God's Word to your rules of conduct. Since God is the author of rules, He must be included in those of your school, or you will not get the results intended.

It is *always* right to do right, it is *never* right to do wrong, and *never* wrong to do right.

Obedience and Honor

When I presented my devotional to our Christian school Board of Trustees on teaching children to have a moral compass, I discussed one of the most important requirements God has of us, which is obedience and honor. God requires parents to train, teach, and discipline children, and gives a lot of passages on how to do so, but He basically gives only one requirement directly to children. It is simple, direct, and to the point. We find it in several places in scripture, but let's look at one of them in Ephesians 6:1-3: "Children, obey your parents in the Lord, for this is right. "HONOR YOUR FATHER AND MOTHER," which is the first commandment with promise: "THAT IT MAY BE WELL WITH YOU AND YOU MAY LIVE LONG ON THE EARTH.""

Christian parents (and also for this discussion, teachers and Christian school administrators) are accountable to God. God is your boss. He is in charge of you. We all submit to Him and to His authority. We are to *obey* God, and to *honor* God. The word *obey* in this context means to learn what God says, and to do what He says. We are to obey Him in all we say and do. We are to obey Him in how we raise our kids in the teachings, nurture, and admonition of Him. The word *honor* means several things, but here are the main meanings for us: We have His name on us (Christian), so we are to act as His representative, and to act as He does. We are to not do anything that would dishonor His name, or make Him look bad. Honor means we highly value God, and we highly respect God.

Honor means we live according to His rules, and not break them, even if we don't like or disagree with some of them. We completely and whole-heartedly trust God, even if we do not know why or do not agree with what He is doing or allowing to happen to us. We know God loves us more than we can imagine, and we know He wants the very best for us. We know God can see a "bigger picture" of our life and we trust He will guide us to, or cause all things to work together for the best result. We have a proper and respectful attitude toward God. Honor means we do not denigrate His name, we do not talk bad about Him, or let others do. Honor means to defend Him – sometimes at great cost to us.

Most little kids don't have a concept of God, they cannot see Him, nor can they read His Word to understand Him. But they do see parents. Parents are the tangible pseudo "God" to them. Parents and teachers are who they are to obey and honor. (Please don't think I am implying we parents or teachers are God – stay with me here) God tells children to obey parents. The concept God has here, which is absolutely brilliant, is that when they learn to obey and honor the parents they can see, then when they mature, they will obey and honor the God cannot see. So there is a period of time in their life when their obedience and honor to God is directly manifested in their obedience and honoring of their parents. In other words, God is in charge of parents, and parents are in charge of their children.

So let's re-do the prior paragraph about parents' relationship to God, writing it again as the children's relationship to parents:

Children (students), you are accountable to your parents. Your parents are your boss. Parents are in charge of you. You submit to them and to their authority. You *obey* your parents, and you *honor* your parents. Obeying means to learn what their rules and expectations of you are, and to do what they say. You are to obey them in all they say and do. You are to obey them because they are ordered by God to raise and train you in the teachings, nurture and admonition of God. God will hold your parents accountable to Him for how they raise you in the teachings, nurture, and admonition of the Him. Honor means several things: You kids have your parents' name on you (probably your last name), so you are to act as their representative when they are not around, to act as God requires you to act. You are not to do anything that would dishonor your parents, or make them look bad. You are to highly value your parents. You are to highly respect your parents. Honor means you live according to their rules, and not break them, even if you don't like some of them, or disagree with some of them. You always and wholeheartedly trust them. They love you more than you can imagine, and they want the best for you. Trust them even if you don't understand why they are requiring something of you, because they know you very well, and they can see the "bigger picture" for you and how things will work out later in your life. Honor means you have a proper and respectful attitude toward your parents, always. Honor means you do not make them look bad. You do not talk bad about Him, nor let others do. Honor means to defend them – even if that means you may lose a friend or may be called names. God is still in charge of you, and you are still to obey and honor God, but the main way you do that is by obeying and honoring your parents. God commands you to do so. Eventually you will be on your own, and you will then obey and honor God directly. However, the passage still applies to all of your life. You are still to honor your parents in the ways mentioned above. This means even when they get old and need you as you need them now. ALWAYS honor your parents as long as they are alive, and even after they are gone.

Another element of that passage in Ephesians is to remember it is taken from one of the Ten Commandments. It is the first commandment that governs our relationships. It sets the best way for families to operate. It is God's plan, and it is a perfect plan that works. In addition to that, it is the first commandment with a promise: A good, fulfilling, and long life. Since God said this, then we must assume He means that obeying and honoring our parents brings honor to God, and He will reward us with a long life, and as long as we keep this commandment, our life will be a good life filled with God's blessings.

God uses the words obey, and honor in the same passage because they go hand-in-hand, you show honor by obeying, and your obedience honors who you obey.

Obeying God means obeying His Word. Reading the Scriptures daily to students is paramount in Christian education. Select texts appropriate for the topics at hand to show the Bible is applicable to everything. I know this takes a little more work preparing your daily lessons, but to God, it is most important. So teachers, please place that kind of priority on weaving God's Word into your lessons, including explaining them and how they are appropriate to the lessons of that day. Jesus, as well as the writers of the New Testament, wove scripture passages into their teaching, please do likewise.

Teach students to obey God's Word:

- No matter what.
- No matter when.
- No matter where.
- No matter who.

Repentance

Another element of this section that is a MUST for a sound Christian school is repentance. If a situation in your school is disciplinary, then repentance is required for resolution, forgiveness, closure, learning, and advancement. The Bible clearly teaches that repentance must be taught, and is a requirement of true humility, true forgiveness, and ultimately true salvation. (Luke 24:47, 2 Corinthians 7:10 to mention just a few) Some churches minimize this teaching, but that does not negate its requirement. Recall a previous statement about pride? Recall that I think it is the root of all sin? If it is the root of sin, then pride must be really hated by

God. Genuine repentance is totally devoid of pride. If we are to have salvation from the penalty of sin, and to be without sin in the eyes of God, there must be true repentance of sin. Taking that to the disciplinary situation with a student, if the child is to learn and move forward, they must repent of their wrongdoing.

Let's get back to teaching the process of how to make decisions (notice I used the term "process", and keep that in mind), where I suggested that after a period of explaining "why" to the younger child, then as they grow, encourage the child to explain in their own words to you "why". Being able to consider "why", or to reflect "why" must be taught and exercised. When teaching a topic or subject, pause for a moment, and ask the student or class "why do you need to learn this"? Or, "why is this important to know". "Why" sometimes is a segway to the next topic or subject, as the lesson may build on the previous lesson, and moving on cannot occur until the previous "why" is known.

In a disciplinary situation, ask the child "why is this wrong?" If appropriate, ask them to give their answer as the reason why and what they think the consequence would be. This teaches them the valuable thought process which also develops their moral compass. School age students are not very good at thinking things through. That is mostly because their mind has not developed enough to process that kind of linear thought or play out a scenario in their mind. So please understand that and have patience with them, but still work with them to develop their disciplined thought process. Teach them to ask themselves "If I do this, what will happen?" "Is this choice what God would want me to do?" Those kinds of quick assessments in the student's mind need to be taught, rehearsed, practiced, and reinforced. It is that thought process that will make repentance of wrongdoing much more palatable.

When teaching repentance, explain to the students it is much more than "I am sorry". (Don't even use the term "sorry", use the term "repent", it is more accurate, and more biblical, especially in a Christian school!) The repentant person is not only sorry for their wrong doing, but they genuinely regret doing it, and will do all they can to not do it again. To use a military term, they do an "about face" and turn 180 degrees and walk away from doing it again. Repentance must be genuine, and needs to be done internally, in the student's heart, and outwardly, by stating it to the offended person. Repentance is necessary for forgiveness, and to have their "slate wiped clean."

Encourage immediate repentance. The sooner the child can come to the understanding of their wrong behavior, repent, forgive, learn from the situation and move on, the better for all involved. Review Psalm 51 where David realized his sins and repented. Several phrases stand out to me in that passage, and one in particular is that although David sinned against several people, he realized in verse 4 that he sinned against God. That concept has to be taught and understood with your students. Repentance must occur to those offended, AND to God. Thanks to Jesus, reconciliation comes from Him, and God actually sees us as He sees Jesus – sinless and righteous. The first few verses of Romans 5 and 1 John 2 explain this.

Repentance was so important to Jesus, that when He officially began His ministry here on earth, he began with the word **Repent!** (Matthew 4:17)

Teach what sin is to your students including the origin of sin in Genesis 3, the penalty of sin, the fact we all sin, the need for repentance and why, and that Jesus has taken away the penalty of sin if the person repents and believes Jesus did. What is sin? Sin is a transgression against God or one of His laws.

When John Wesley went to college, his mother wrote a letter to him with a definition of sin: "Take this rule: whatever weakens your reason, impairs the tenderness of your conscience, obscures your sense of God, or takes off your relish of spiritual things; in short, whatever increases the strength and authority of your body over your mind, that thing is sin to you, however innocent it may be in itself." - Susanna Wesley June 8, 1725

Discipline

"And it is good for people to submit at an early age to the yoke of his discipline." Lamentations 3:27 NLT

Rules of conduct for your students, and discipline for when those rules are not followed is an integral part of learning, it teaches children that there are consequences resulting from their actions, teaches them to make proper decisions, to have self-control, and then the learned ability of self-discipline.

Understanding that God's Word says children (and all people) have by nature a tendency to sin is pivotal to the approach of teaching, training, and disciplining children. (Jeremiah 17:9, Galatians 5:16-21, Ephesians 2, Romans 3:23 & 5:8-15) Discipline is biblical, and some Bible passages even give us a specific method and location to apply discipline: (Proverbs 10:13, 13:24, 19:18, 22:15 & 17, 23:13-14, 26:3, and 29:15). Our society has greatly changed in the acceptable methods of discipline over the past twenty years or so. Corporal punishment (physical spanking) as described in the Bible passages above are not only frowned upon in our culture these days, but some parents and possibly even schools have been charged with child abuse or similar charges as a result of properly administered spanking. Because biblical discipline is required of parents from a loving and just God, the results of not disciplining children His way are showing up in society today as alcoholism, drug abuse, crime, apathy, selfishness, disrespect for others, etc. I believe Satan has orchestrated this movement to abolish corporal punishment because he knows it is a key part of Gods plan of training children and he knows (and wants) the detrimental results the lack of this discipline has on society. As best as you can, don't fall for Satan's plan.

To properly train children in the nurture and admonition of the Lord (Ephesians 6:4), Christian schools and Home Schools need to have a set policy on discipline. I will not outline one here, because most all schools (and parents) have wrestled with this issue and arrived at their own policy. The process of developing a policy through biblical research, prayer, and wise council, is an effort you or your school MUST go through so you can stand on that foundation with confidence, and explain it to parents and students (or your own children) confidently as well.

Never discipline in anger. Always discipline in love. Yes, doing so in love will be hard at the time, and certainly the student being disciplined at the time will have a hard time believing it is out of love, but it should be true. Hebrews 12:5-8 talks about a loving father disciplines his son, and the opposite is true also (not disciplining a child correctly shows a lack of love). The wisest man in history (Solomon) said the same thing in Proverbs 3:11-12. Then, in Hebrews 12:11 the writer says discipline is painful at the time, but if done correctly, results in "the peaceable fruit of righteousness to those who have been trained by it."

Discipline that is effective must be done from a well thought out, biblical, and firm policy, and be carried out *consistently.* Inconsistent discipline can be detrimental to a child, and can lead to confusion and then rebellion. Your policy, and the people responsible for carrying out the discipline per that policy, must have these biblical characteristics: justice, two-way open communication, grace, forgiveness, and love. When disciplinary action is taken toward a student, always point out and explain what God says in scripture about the offense, and the underlying sin. Remember to verify sources of the accusation and/or offense, and try to have two or three witnesses as 1 Timothy 5:19 mentions (although not specifically toward sin or accusations in students, it is a good policy to maintain).

Now, with that all said, let me simplify it and say treat the student with C.A.R.E.:

Communication. Connect with the student in a way that he/she understands your authority, and also that you care deeply about them and their growth from the situation. Be sure to listen to the student, it is a two-way conversation. (Romans 13:1-5; Proverbs 13:14)

Assessing the situation such as why this happened, who was involved (if appropriate) what started the situation and their thinking process, when did this happen, and was it a quick response or a well thought out devious plan. Your intention here is to get to the student's heart of the matter, because their heart is what you will be correcting. (Proverbs 18:13,17, 20:5, Luke 6:45, Psalm 139:23-24)

Repentance is the goal, from their heart, which means accepting and understanding the wrong that was committed, the sin involved, the need for repentance, and the understanding of not doing it again. Grace and Truth must be included, but also explain the disciplinary action and why it must occur. (Proverbs 13:24, 22:15, Hebrews 4:16, 12:11, John 1:14, 1 John 1:9)

Encouragement is how to end each situation where the student is encouraged of God's, and your love for them. They have learned to be a better person in God's eyes because of this situation, and that they are forgiven and are leaving with a restored heart that is encouraged to live for Jesus, who is the center of their view of themself and others. (Galatians 6:1-2, John 15, Hebrews 3:12-15)

There is a school Principal who has a specific chair in his office that he calls the "Hot Seat". When a student is in trouble, he is sent to the Principals office and told to sit in that seat. I got to thinking about that, and would like to suggest it be called the "CARE Chair". Maybe he even put the word "C.A.R.E." above the chair as a reminder of how to treat the student/situation. I also am reminded of a saying that is somewhat relative here: "They won't care how much you know until they know how much you care."

Discipline done incorrectly can tear students down, demoralize them, and/or possibly even turn them away from God's Truth. When disciplining a student, make sure the offense is understood, the disciplinary action agreed to, and afterwards, reassure the student of their value, your love for them, God's love for them, your forgiveness of the offense, and if they repented, you expect them not to repeat the offense. If need be, build them back up, because the goal is "the peaceable fruit of righteousness to those who have been trained by it". As you develop your policy, keep in mind the statement that **discipline is an integral component of learning, of self-control,**

of a moral compass, of character building, of training the heart, and therefore an element of a sound Christian school.

Self-Discipline

"Self-discipline does not come from self, it must be taught to self, and then self-performed". I mentioned that statement to a frustrated single parent with whom I was having a conversation. She was thinking of not letting him finish his senior year at the Christian grade school he has been attending for 6 years. His grades had steadily plummeted and his GPA was now at 1.75. Yet, he had just taken his college entrance ACT test for the first time, and scored a 28, which is extremely high. I can understand her frustration due to the disparity in those two indicators.

"Self-discipline is the boy's main problem" I told her, not the school. She agreed and commented that his low grades are a result of frequently not turning in homework, (even if he had it completed) forgetting assignments, not preparing for tests, etc. However, if you create a controlled and monitored environment, such as taking the ACT test, his intellectual abilities shine impressively; further proving a lack of self-discipline. His Mom had never taught him how to be self-disciplined, and neither had any teachers at his school. Self-discipline has to be taught, and I do not mean taught to have it, because it is not something you have, but is something you do. It is a habit you have to learn with practice. God knew self-discipline was something very difficult for us, but very much needed. Not that He created a flaw in us, but that similar to talking, we have to learn it and learn it well, which takes practice. When we learn it, we can then be most effective for Him.

There is great news for us though: God helps us to be self-disciplined, so much so, that it is one of the three *special powers* we have as Christians, which are found in 2 Timothy 1:7 "For God has not given us a spirit of fear, but of power and of love and of a sound mind." The third special power or mental disposition God has given us in that verse is a "sound mind", which is actually one word in the original Greek manuscript, meaning "to be self-controlled and disciplined". We have to put forth the effort, and do the hard work and practice to be self-disciplined. And, since God wants us to be self-disciplined, we *will* be if we do our part. Proverbs 25:28 says without self-discipline, we are like a city that is broken down, and without walls for protection, and you can bet God does not want us to be like that.

During my conversation with that single Mom about her son, I asked her to come up with household rules and duties to teach her son to be self-disciplined. Those include completing homework prior to watching television, playing video games, or anything else. Place completed homework in his backpack, and put it by the door so he would not forget it. Also, he should be rewarded for deeds involving self-discipline, and reprimanded (disciplined, such as taking away some privileges) for lack of self-discipline. The idea is to train correctly to produce good habits, and good habits result in good character. Schools should similarly come up with methods to teach students self-discipline. Remember, kids are to be trained, and self-discipline is something needing to be trained.

One other thing I mentioned to the single Mom was the passage in 2 Timothy says God gives us the *spirit* of power, love, and self-discipline. That does refer to the Holy Spirit, who dwells in us when we are a true Christian. The Holy Spirit will help us to have those three. So if we Christians do not have a mental disposition of power, love, and self-discipline, then what spirit do we have? That is a very serious question! Yes, I asked that single Mom to sit down with her son, and tenderly explain that to him, and to ensure he really is a true Christian. Because as Paul also said in Galatians 5:22-23, one of the fruits of the Spirit, is self-control!

> *"Sow a thought and you reap an action; sow an act and you reap a habit; sow a habit and you reap a character; sow a character and you reap a destiny."* –Ralph Waldo Emerson

Character Building

"Maintain good character." I tell that to my daughter nearly every day as a reminder, especially whenever she leaves to a friend's house, the mall, or a school trip. It is an accountability issue with her too, because I will often ask her when she returns home if she maintained good character, and ask for some examples. You may ask: how does she know what good character is? Well, we have taught her. She didn't just acquire it, because with the sinful nature in us all (we Christians know what that means), good character has to be taught and learned. Does your school do a good job of teaching good character? Do you have specific lessons in the classroom to teach good character? The next several paragraphs will be examples of how to teach good character to students.

Character comes from the inside out; it is the outward expression of the inner heart, and is rooted in biblical principles. Those principles must be taught because they are not from our natural self. Attitude is an indication of character, so think of the attitude of students you know or teach, and how that is a reflection of their character. How do you handle differing attitudes in students? Do you chastise bad attitudes, and praise good attitudes? I would suggest that you come up with some specific lessons and rewards for the topic of character. You should also use opportunities in the classroom to point out examples of good, and bad character both in the topics of discussion (when studying Joseph, George Washington, General MacArthur, or Judas Iscariot, Nero, or Bernie Madoff) or when a student demonstrates good or bad character at school. Using examples is one way to teach good character. Be sure to reinforce each character example with passages from Scripture.

Teachers, staff, and parents should always be a model of good character. How are you doing in that? In a classroom situation, a school or sporting event, or in front of kids or God, how are you always demonstrating good character? Pay attention to that, students are watching, and learning from you!

The closer you are to God, the more of His character attributes you see, such as His faithfulness, generosity, hatred for sin, lovingkindness, mercy, grace, and His sovereignty. The closer to God you are, the more of His character attributes you take on for yourself as well!

The closer a sound Christian school is to God, the more of His character attributes the school has, and the more visible they are to others.

My Father used to tell me: "Your true character comes out when no one is looking". That is an important statement to instill in your students. Remember character is something in a student that has to be taught to them, and they have to learn it, and work on it. Be careful how you portray character, however, and think carefully about how you teach it. For instance, I remember my Dad saying right before a spanking "Here comes the belt of character", and another time, when I was told to clean the manure out of our barn "This job will teach you some character". I don't know how those helped me build character, and I probably learned the wrong meaning of the word, so be careful of that, but my Dad is a wise man, there must have been a reason. I do know proper discipline and communicating the reasons why the student is being disciplined teaches good character. So ask God to give you wisdom in how you discipline and teach character to students.

Teaching character to students should emulate how God teaches us. He does so using His Word, He is merciful toward us, patient with us, gives us a lot of grace, is persistent with us, uses trials suffering to teach us, and helps us learn from our mistakes. He does not demand perfection, but wants us to strive toward it. He does not burden us with rules, but has rules for our own good (we can tend to use a lot of rules in an attempt to please Him, which is called legalism, which he was upset at the Pharisees over). He understands we mess up, but grants repentance, mercy, and forgiveness, and asks us to humbly try again in the direction of righteousness. Oh, and remember to "lighten up". God is not a kill-joy, he wants us to be joyful, and to remember He loves us more than we will ever know.

One essential method of teaching character to students is by using the acronym T.E.A.C.H., which is Thinking, Emotions, Actions, Character, and Honor. Here is how it works:

Whenever any situation comes up in life such as a decision to be made, or a response to some sort of a stimulant such as harsh words spoken to the person, or an occurrence such as a change of plans or another driver cuts you off, there is a process that takes place:

- **Thinking**. A person must think what their reaction will be to the situation or stimulant. This is the proper first step, and it takes self-discipline to do this. This first step usually does not come naturally; it has to be taught to students. Most everyone's reaction to a stimulant begins with the second step (emotions), but thinking must occur prior to an emotional response. Thinking how to handle the situation biblically is the goal here, so use biblical examples when teaching this.
- **Emotions**. In nearly all situations, your thoughts are to control your emotions. That statement is hard to do; therefore it must be taught and understood by the student. God created emotions, and they are wonderful. However, improper emotions, and uncontrolled emotions can be detrimental to the person and to others. Reacting to a "bad" situation or occurrence can, by our (sinful) nature, almost always evokes emotions such as anger, worry, or fear, which are all sins according to God's Word. Learning to control those bad emotions at the onset of the situation is a must, and then think about it logically, rationally, and biblically.
- **Actions**. This is the acting out of your thinking or your emotions. We can all recite a sad situation where a person's emotional reaction (action) to a situation was not good.

We can also recall how impressed we were when a person handled a situation thoughtfully with actions of grace and good character (biblically). Students need to be taught to react to a situation by pausing and thinking about that situation, how they will respond, and how they can glorify God in their response.

- **Character.** A person's character is defined and displayed by how they handle a situation. Their actions will generally show their true character, which comes from how they thoughtfully or emotionally deal with a situation. As a person matures, the process a person goes through in their mind prior to their action becomes quicker, and more natural. So have patience with students as they work on this.
- **Honor.** Just as a person's character is defined by the acting out of their thinking and emotions, a person's honor is defined by their character. Honor is the outpouring of your character on others, and God, as well as yourself. It is what other people, and God, think of you. Honor is something you have to pretty much constantly work on. You work on it by solidifying your beliefs, having confidence in your beliefs, and then using those beliefs in the process of thinking about a situation and your reaction to it, controlling your emotions in that situation, and by acting responsibly to the situation. When a person acts honorably, they bring honor to God.

Remember most people react to a stimulating situation by bypassing thinking and going straight to emotions. And, most of the time, the results are less than desirable. Jesus handled every stimulating situation by thinking first, and His thoughts were controlled by His "biblical" knowledge and wisdom, and so should we. So if you are a teacher or parent, teach that to students. How do you teach this? By using T.E.A. The proper steps to reacting to every stimulating situation is in this specific order: Thinking, Emotions, Actions. First you think about the stimulant and carefully consider your reaction, including the effects of your reaction. Then let emotions help with your decision (get fired up about it, or calm down about it), then your carefully thought out actions occur responding to the stimulant. Most of you can probably say those steps are opposite of how most people handle stimulating situations, and agree the results are rarely good. There are a lot of Bible passages that support this, my favorite is 1 Peter 1:13-16 which says to think clearly and exercise self-control, a few others are Proverbs 13:16, 16:32, 25:28, 29:11, Galatians 5:16-24, 2 Peter 1:5-8.

Teach the self-discipline of pausing briefly, take a step back in the mind and look at the situation as a whole, ask "what would please Jesus"? Sometimes playing out different scenarios in your mind can be good, if the student can do that, but most kids have trouble processing things that way in their mind. In any situation it is good to ask, does this please Jesus, or does it please self? It is **always** best to please Jesus, which is better than any fleeting pleasure or satisfaction that He would not approve of.

Ed Welch, a Christian Author and Biblical Counselor wrote: "When principles or steps wander from Christ himself, they become self-serving guidelines. They make our marriages, families, friendships, and work go better, but the goal is our own betterment more than the glory of God… 'Be good' and 'Do right' are fine messages, but when they stand alone they have more in common with the Boy Scouts' Handbook than Scripture. Remember that in the Bible, 'This is who God is and what He has done' always precedes 'this is what you must do.' Action follows our knowledge of God and trust in Him. It is as if God has said to us, 'Now that you have seen who I am, you will want to love Me in return…'"[29] Character is patterned after God's Word, and our character grows more pleasing to Him when the more like Jesus we become.

Here is another "character" saying I have told my daughter: "Try to find sunshine even on a cloudy day, the sun is always there, some days you just have to strive a little harder to see it." That goes well with the biblical command in Philippians 4 to "rejoice always".

A person with good character is optimistic, filled with hope, joy, and peace. I also like to give this spelling and definition to her… "Sonshine: The light of God's Son Jesus shining through us. How will you be sonshine today?" I wrote that on a yellow sticky note and put it on her school things one day. Several years later, that same sticky note is on her main notebook that she sees every school day.

Sound Christian schools teach the biblical process of handling situations of life, which begins by thinking controlling emotions.

To reiterate: character is an attribute that has to be taught to students, and they *must learn* it. So teach the process of possessing proper character to your students. Teach application, not just implication. Teach the meaning of these words that instill, and demonstrate good character: Wisdom, gracious, patience, self-discipline, gentleness, trustworthiness, purity, others-centered, diligence, punctuality, generosity, honesty, perseverance, compassion, courageous, and hard working. Notice those words can also describe some character traits of God. Maybe that is why Paul said in Romans 8:29 we are to endeavor to become like Jesus! Along with those great words of good character go two other attributes that must be taught and learned: Confidence, and Value.

Confidence comes from having a firm faith or belief in what is right, proper, and effective. Make sure you teach that belief to them, and of course, that belief comes through Jesus and the Bible. Confidence comes from being told *well done*. Reinforce the confidence of students by making sure they are acknowledged or rewarded for a job well done, and are built back up after correction or discipline.

Value is another trait that you must teach your students. God loves them no matter what. There is nothing they can do that will diminish God's love of them, and there is nothing they can do that will cause God to love them more. (He may be disappointed, or on the other hand be pleased, but His love never waivers). Teachers should also have that same attitude toward their students. Teaching a student they are valuable is a must. Every person wants to have value, and Christian education should ensure each and every student has value, especially during the teen years when they are struggling to understand their value, and look for it in various places: so be one of the places that they feel secure and valued. Be very clear, a person's value or self-worth comes from God not _______(fill in the blank with what is appropriate).

In developing a policy on discipline, as recently mentioned, a sound Christian school also incorporates a policy on character building that includes the processes of handling a stimulating situation, confidence, and value. Teaching the student to make godly choices on their own is the goal. The story of Joseph in Genesis can be a great example to use as a basis of your policy. There is also a wealth of information on-line about teaching character. Your school may use such tools as encouraging or requiring volunteerism or community service from students, offer a "Christian Character Award" in sports and the classroom, or spotlight specific examples of Christian character stories of students in a school publication or bulletin board. I encourage you to research those and purposefully administer a character building policy for your Christian school.

Rules of conduct, why those rules exist, explanation and understanding when rules are broken, humble repentance of specific wrongdoing, properly explaining why and administering discipline, reconciliation with love, accountability to ensure non-repeating the wrongdoing, praise when correction and proper attitude is recognized, and the resultant character building is a biblical process that is part of a sound Christian school.

Chapter 12

School Vision, Plan, and Goals

"Come up with a plan, and then work that plan" is a statement made often by Bill Zimmerman, a great leader in the steel fabrication business. I never worked for Bill, but know several people who did, and they kept using his statement in many areas of their career and personal lives. It applies to Christian education as well. Think of a road trip in your car; you plan your route, and only deviate from that route if absolutely necessary, and after that brief deviation, you get back on your planned route to your destination. Without a planned out course to take, you will wander aimlessly, get off course, expend unneeded effort or fuel, travel on bumpy roads, and possibly even get stuck in mud, only to be late or never get to your destination. Similarly, Christian schools need a planned course, or consequences will occur.

The Dream, the Vision, the Plan

When planning for the future, Proverbs 16:3 and 9 come to mind: "Commit your works to the LORD, and your thoughts will be established…A man's heart plans his way, but the LORD directs his steps." God gave you a brain, so use it. Keep your focus on the Lord, and His Word, prayerfully and decidedly establish your schools vision and plan, and He will direct your steps along that plan. I hear too often of people with no plan aimlessly bumbling through life, or life's situations saying something like "God will show me what to do", or "God will take care of me", or "God will direct my steps". Although those are true statements by themselves, in context an analogy would be going outside without a coat when it is 30 degrees below zero and saying "God will take care of me." Don't put God in a situation like that. God gave you a brain; use it to plan, and plan ahead.

School leaders should have a vision for their school, and a plan to accomplish that vision. Here is a sequential list of steps for coming up with your school's plan:

- *Brainstorm* for ideas.
- Give *reasons* for those ideas.
- Write a *plan* to accomplish those ideas.
- Choose *goals* or milestones of accomplishing those ideas.
- *Celebrate* attaining those goals.
- *Review* the plan.
- Revise if necessary, and *continue.*

Here is an expanded look at each step:

1) The leaders of the school sit down in a *brainstorming* session (you could call it a Strategic Planning Session), and make two short lists:

   List one is the short term dreams, ideas, or goals for your school. Ask "what do we want to change or accomplish in 3 years." Write those down, prioritize them, and arrive at a list.

   List two is long term dreams, ideas, or goals, so ask "what do we want our school to look like in 12 or maybe 15 years". Keep in mind, that many short term ideas or goals are stepping stones toward long term ideas or goals.

All successful people had a dream. Martin Luther King Jr.'s fame was based on one statement, a statement that fostered reasons, gave excitement, gave purpose, and gave inspiration to an oppressed group of people: "I have a dream..." All successful companies had a dream. Microsoft had a dream "A computer on every desk." Ford had a dream: "Making the automobile affordable." Have you seen the movie "Tucker, a Man and His Dream?" Some suggestions of ideas you may come up with are to increase your enrollment by a certain percentage, or establish and fund a financial aid program, or add a girls' volleyball team, or hire a Guidance Counselor, or add new classrooms, or cut overhead costs by a certain percentage. Whatever ideas you come up with, be specific.

2) Now that you have those two lists, write down next to each item the *reasons* you want to accomplish those ideas. A famous saying is "If you have enough reasons, you can accomplish the most incredible things!" Therefore *reasons* are a source of inspiration. Everything starts with an idea, it is driven by reasons, then solutions will follow.
3) How are you going to achieve those ideas? The reasons you wrote down will motivate you, but you need a *plan*. This is the hard part, but buck up and write down how you think you will accomplish the ideas you have. Get serious about it, don't just hope, poor people hope, successful people are serious and make a plan to achieve their hopes. If you fail to plan, you are planning to fail. Read your plan several times and refine it, then settle on it. You are then ready to work it. You can change it if you absolutely need to, but the idea is to get a plan and work that plan. Get excited about your plans. Get everyone else excited about the plans. Be a person that shows up Monday morning and says with vigor "Yippie! Another week to work on our plans!"

4) Now, set and write down some *goals* to achieve while working on your plans. Primarily these are calendar dates, but may be percentages of the total, or a quantity to achieve. Without goals, people lose interest, and plans fizzle. How long would you play a game that did not have a goal? To some degree, running a Christian school is similar. So set some realistic and attainable goals. Some call them milestones, but I like the term "goal" because I like football. Picture the goal line or goalpost, and every member of the team planning, motivating, and striving go get to that goal. They celebrate when they reach that goal, and don't quit there, but regroup, and do it again.
5) So *celebrate* when you reach a goal! Have a pizza luncheon or donuts in the morning. Then regroup, and head for the next goal. Don't set the goal too high, and don't set it too low (too high and disillusionment sets in, too low and you run out of pizza money). If you find while working toward the goal that it seems too high, move it lower (or visa-versa). A good leader will ascertain the situation, and decide if the motivation is waning, and give hope and excitement by moving the goal if needed (either way).
6) Set dates for *reviewing* your plans as they progress. Ask questions such as "how are we progressing?", "Are we still on track for our goal?", "Is there anything we should be doing different?", and "Is there any improvements we can make to the plan or goal?" Also, review your plans after you have achieved them (or didn't). Learn from your mistakes, or you will repeat them again, or learn from your achievements and multiply them. Become goal oriented. Become plan driven. Going back to the football metaphor, the team huddles up between plays. So get your staff together regularly and discuss the plan, and strategy. Ask how everyone is doing in their part toward achieving the goal. Halfway through

the school year, do this on a more formal basis just like the football team goes into the locker room at halftime and the coach and players discuss how the strategy is working, and what changes need to be made to accomplish the goals.

7) "Rinse and repeat" the shampoo directions say. Clean up your mistakes or unproductive endeavors, and do another plan right away. Make vision planning and achievement a part of your school's routine. Maybe have an annual school vision retreat where the plan(s) for achieving the vision of the school is the only topic. Discuss accomplishments, and failures. Plan how to remedy the failures. Discuss and implement new dreams or ideas. Never forget though, just like a football team, there is a coach. That coach is in charge of the overall plan, and uses the players to carry out that plan. As in Proverbs 16 mentioned earlier, that coach is the LORD. Before each huddle, the quarterback looks at or runs to the coach. Do that often, look to the LORD and His Word for direction, encouragement, and maybe correction.

I know of schools and home schools that have a theme each semester or school year. That theme could be tied to the school goals. Getting the whole school excited about the theme can be fun and rewarding, and draws focus to the goals and plan of the school, as well as get more people involved in praying for, and accomplishing the goals.

A sound Christian school has specific vision, plan, and the means to accomplish that vision, through the Lord and His Word.

Chapter 13

Fundraising and Donations

Some Christian schools charge higher tuition fees, and place minimal effort toward fundraising and receive few donations; while other schools try to keep tuition as low as possible and make up the difference from donations and fundraising. I believe Christian schools should be between those two, but lean more toward fundraising and donations because it provides an opportunity for blessing, unity, and spreading the Gospel.

Fundraising for your Christian school is a difficult, yet honorable endeavor. You need to have faith and trust that God will provide for your school, and at the same time, you are to expend a sufficient amount of effort to fundraising so as to accomplish the goals and needs of the school. In essence, God will open the doors, but you need to find the doors and go through them. You need to also have in mind that while God blesses your school with gifts from others, He will also bless the giver, so part of your mindset is to provide the opportunity for others to serve God in their giving, and hopefully to be blessed in return.

Fundraising presents a platform opportunity for unity. Study Philippians 1:27 through 2:11 and relate it to your school fundraising efforts. Parents, various church members, retired people, and local businesses all can participate in your Christian school in some sort of a "family" atmosphere of unity through fundraising. What makes fundraising difficult is when few participate. Usually what happens is a couple of energetic and dedicated parents seem to have the fundraising burden dumped on them and they get burned out and a sour attitude about fundraising ensues (to the detriment of the school). Be mindful of that happening, and guard against it by giving those folks a break, rotate fundraising event participation, set realistic goals, and try to get more people involved. Every school will have people who want to help with fundraising, and people who do not. That is alright, but at the onset of enrolling in your school, people need to know fundraising needs to occur and the more people that are involved, the more the school can be blessed, the less costly tuition could be, and the more "family" atmosphere of unity there can be at the school.

We Christians are to be in the world not of the world (John 17). "In the world" means we are not to be separatists, but be out there in the world shining as light in the darkness, presenting and living the Gospel of Christ. Fundraising is a great vehicle to get out there "in the world", to present the Gospel to others, and for others to see Jesus Christ in us. It is a way to shine like lights, and for people to learn what your school is about, stands for, and does for society, and to erode any fallacies people may have about your school. Look at fundraising as a way of witnessing, and God will bless your efforts because it is His desire that all be saved.

Fundraising will only be honoring to God if you are good stewards of what you have raised with the full mindset that God has given it to your school, so use it as God wants it to be used. Integrity before your God is the key here, and not only the integrity and good stewardship of the school, but of each person involved in the school administration of funds as well. If your personal life is not fully pleasing to the Lord with your good stewardship (and your generous giving), your handling of donations and tuition money will not be either. Don't allow your school to be in situations that are not pleasing to the Lord, nor *appear* unpleasing to Him. Your donors are watching, God's reputation is at stake.

Specifying needs:

One of the typical shortcomings of fundraising in Christian schools is that people do not know the needs of the school. A lot of people are not very willing to give to the general fund of your school, but they would like to give to a specific need they could identify with. This identification is important because it gives purpose to the donor and also gives them a specific prayer topic. An example is a couple whose children have grown, yet still wanted to donate to our local Christian school. They wanted to specifically donate to help a family with multiple children so they could afford to send *all* their kids to the school. To the recipient family, it was an *anonymous* donation, but to the donor, they had a specific family in need they were helping to support financially as well as prayerfully. I also know of an employee of a construction specialties supply company whose owner did not want to support the Christian school financially, but did allow a donation of a basketball backboards when he found out the school needed new ones. So make specific needs of your school known.

Several years ago God graciously fulfilled a dream of mine, which was to build my own house for my family. I had a house type and floor plan in mind since my days in college when I worked part time building houses, so I knew what I wanted. While in college, the home construction crew I worked for did most every aspect of building the house, from forming and pouring the concrete foundation, to framing, electrical, plumbing, drywall, and roofing. However, when we purchased the land and began the building process as I did in college, it became painfully clear that this was an overwhelming endeavor. So I broke down the construction process into smaller disciplines such as framing, electrical, siding, roofing, etc. It enabled one overwhelming big task to seem like smaller manageable ones. I also delegated some tasks to more experienced people such as plumbing, and a couple tasks I knew I did not have time to do such as drywall tape and texturing. Do that with your fundraising endeavors.

To be good stewards, and to let people know the needs of your school, you need to define and structure your fundraising needs and endeavors into these three categories: **Operational**, **Growth, Scholarships,** and **Ministry**.

Operational needs are the general funds needed to operate the school. This is outlined in the general budget of the school. Additionally, many budget items have a budgeted amount that is lower than should be. Listing those items and what you would like those budgeted amounts to actually be would provide folks with a list of items they could help fund.

Growth needs are contained in two sub categories, which are the needs of **committed** and **uncommitted** growth. A new building addition is a committed growth need. Uncommitted growth items are *wish list* items that are not committed to be purchased at the present time. Planning for future growth, future remodeling, future replacements, even items on a wish list outside of the current budget or committed growth are all part of uncommitted growth needs. The Growth needs of your school should be itemized and then categorized into either committed, or uncommitted. Then, those two lists should be prioritized with what is most needed at the top of the list.

Scholarship needs are simply to help people who cannot afford to enroll their kids at your Christian school. If a parent has prayerfully decided in their heart that they want a Christ based education is for their kid(s), then God will provide the financial means for them and scholarships are the main means. There are full scholarships, and there are partial scholarships, and those are to be accorded with the prioritized needs of families. We are instructed biblically to care for widows and orphans, so children who have lost one or both parents should rise to the top of the priority list. Then we should help those that are less fortunate financially. However, we must maintain an attitude of helping people who work hard, but just simply cannot afford all or part of the tuition. Be mindful not to help, enable, or reward laziness, lack of biblical morals and/or priorities, or sinful behavior.

Ministry needs are something often overlooked by Christian schools, but still are important. A High School mission's trip is one example of a ministry that your school can be, or is involved with. Community outreach projects, hosting concerts of Christian performers with a Gospel message, supporting specific missionaries, are a few examples of spreading the Gospel that Christian schools could be involved in; many of which needs funding. The Ministry needs should be identified, kept to a few to gain the most support and success, and be made known.

With these organized lists, people can see where the need is and where they would like to help. Remember many people do not give to a general fund, but if they can choose an item or area they like or can connect with, they will be happy to support. Also remember fundraising for your school is providing the opportunity for God to bless the giver, and for Him to be praised.

Now that you have an organized list of needs of your school, we will look at suggested instructions and requirements for funding those needs.

Instructions, Requirements, and Suggestions for Fundraising:

You know your core Christian values concerning your school. Write them down, and use them as the foundation of fundraising efforts, or as pep talk material. You should see such terms written down as: prayer, faith and trust in God, your passion for His purpose and His work in your school, your creativity and ingenuity, your hard work, your good stewardship and accountability, and even your frugality. Your Biblical values should be woven in there also such as honesty, Truth, doing the right thing, and love for others more than self. Make sure they are reviewed prior to, and during all fundraising efforts. If the fundraising endeavor involves your students, it will be an opportunity for them to learn those values and practice them. The likeness of Jesus should come alive during your fundraising ventures.

I would suggest your school designate one person to be in charge of all fundraising efforts; one person that exemplifies Jesus Christ in their life. Since followers tend to be like their leader, you want a person in charge that sets the example of the values you want in your fundraising efforts. This person should wisely choose the endeavors to pursue, being mindful of how your school is perceived through these fundraising ventures. You do not want too many, out of control, undiscerning, poorly planned, poorly executed, or "little return for the effort" fund raising ventures. Those will turn off or burn out parents, supporters, donors, and students, and thwart your fundraising efforts.

Whether your venture is selling chocolate, discount cards, magazines, performing services such as car washes, cleaning homes, or obtaining donations from businesses or even applying for grants, consider each one carefully as to the perception of your school it will create. Remember also to not allow the appearance of evil (1 Thessalonians 5:22). Choose wisely the fundraising campaigns that give the best return for the effort. Choose those that shine a good light on your school and God. Plan them well, execute that plan well, and create and maintain a great level of excitement, hope, and trust in God.

Be sure to utilize the full spectrum of fundraising avenues. Small ventures such as bake sales, car washes, or product sales, will involve students, and you should use these as opportunities to teach the students salesmanship, courtesy, communication skills, presentation, counting money and giving change, thankfulness, etc. Medium to large ventures may be donation based auctions, school garage sales, dinners featuring a famous speaker, or entertainment endeavors. Those all take planning, coordination, and volunteerism. There are wonderful resources found on-line, I would suggest doing a search for "Christian school fundraising". There are also Christian fundraising consultants and coaches who offer various levels of fundraising help. I am somewhat familiar with two such consultants in Colorado which are GraceWorks Ministries, and Dickerson and Associates, but I am sure there are others as well if you do an on-line search for "Christian School Fundraising Consultants". Be sure to review their statement of faith or core values to ensure their basis is biblical, and would align with that of your school. Be diligent at this, and use discernment please, as fundraising is an area of great potential help for your school, or could be harmful to you r school and the name and work of Jesus Christ.

In addition to the suggestions mentioned above, here is specific advice on fundraising, and how to pursue it:

Prayer:

Prayer is *essential* to the growth of Christian schools. Prayer demonstrates faith, a contrite heart, and a purpose that is God-centered. Prayer enables you to focus on God and not so much on yourself. Prayer gives the proper perspective of Gods attributes and character such as His holiness, His power and strength, His Word, His riches, His mercy, and grace. Praying puts into perspective your faith in Him, serving Him, and obeying Him. God wants humble people focused on Him to accomplish His wishes. Here are some suggestions for Prayer concerning your school, some specifically to fundraising:

1) List specific prayer needs or topics on a bulletin board, or weekly newsletter where everyone involved with your school can see and pray about them.

2) Have prayer meetings regularly where folks meet just to pray for the school. Have staff prayer meetings, possibly each morning prior to the start of school. If your school operates with committees devoted to specific topics or issues such as fa undraising committee, begin and end each meeting with prayer. Parents groups, school board, and/or staff should pray for those committees. It is easy to lose focus and get chit chatty, stay on topic and stay on prayer. Colossians 4:2, 1 Thessalonians 5:17, 1 Timothy 2:8.
3) Prior to prayer, spend some time searching for any sins or sinful ways you may have that could be a barrier between you and God. Confess those sins to those offended, and to God, and ask for forgiveness. Then earnestly strive to eradicate the sin(s) and not repeat them. Psalm 26:2, 139:23-24
4) Then, spend some time discussing the many blessings from God concerning your school. Count them one by one if you can. Mention them to each other, and thank God for those blessings, it is a form of praise to Him, as well as setting a correct mindset toward God and focuses on His faithfulness. Psalm 37:3, Philippians 4:6
5) Please pray biblically. I would suggest prayers be structured similar to the prayers of people in the Bible, especially the sample template Jesus outlined for us in Matthew 6. Formality and structure however is not as important as attitude, humbleness, perspective, faith, content, submissiveness of your heart, etc. The "ACTS" acronym is a simple structure I use from time to time: Adoration, Confession, Thanksgiving, and Supplication.
6) Try to focus on what God wants, and the needs of your school from *His* perspective. How does that compare to *your* wants? Remember our purpose includes honoring and obeying God, and to love each other. Pray that God will be honored through your school and your students, and obey

His Word, which includes the commandment to love one another. John 14:15, 15:12

7) Pray individually for your school, and other Christian schools. Many people are involved in Bible studies, or other group meetings where prayer requests are taken and prayed for. Be sure to mention and pray for your Christian school in settings like those.
8) Pray that people become aware of your Christian school and what it offers, and that they would be involved in your school in any meaningful way, including financial support.

Targeting:

You need to identify different groups of donors and target those groups with information and needs of the school specifically tailored to them. This information given to them should explain your school including the *value* and *benefits* of Christian education. Suggested target groups are:

1) Area Churches
    a. Probably our biggest sources of donation help, but typically donate the least.
    b. Draft a letter or brochure with information centered on why the church should financially support your Christian School. Don't refrain from *preaching to the choir* when you outline the biblical reasons for supporting Christian education. The church may want to know that you know the biblical reasons your Christian school exists. They will need to know your school's financial needs whether that means scholarships for students of parents that have trouble paying the tuition, or materials they would support for educating biblically; don't be afraid to highlight

specific areas of need and the amounts you suggest they donate.

c. Ask to place a notice in the church bulletin concerning your school such as a specific upcoming event or fundraiser, or possibly a list of needs.
d. Ask if the School administrator or board President or Chairperson be allowed to speak to their church concerning your school. This may be a presentation to the whole congregation, or to speak to the church board or even the church budget committee to ask for allocation of support funds for your school; the topics depend on the audience.
e. Invite Pastors and Church Elders to visit your school for a personal tour, or invite them to an Open House.

2) Area Businesses
   a. Many area businesses would love to donate to a Christian school. They just do not know of a need. Many assume Christian schools are fully funded by tuition, or fully supported by churches. Many schools are funded that way, but most are not, so let them know how your school is funded, and the need for donations. Identify specific needs tailored to specific businesses, possibly products or capital improvements your school needs that those businesses provide.
   b. Donations should be a write off for businesses and/or a tax deduction, so be sure to let them know that, and that you would be sending them a receipt for that purpose if they would provide the amount. Many donations are not necessarily monetary. Many can donate unsold items, and write off the full cost of these items, and possibly receive more from a tax credit than discounting them for quick sale.
   c. Many businesses are owned by Christians, or have Christians working for them, and may just need to

be informed that they can donate to God's work at a Christian school, just like any other ministry, they just need a little help and direction. Many businesses have an annual budget for donations and community support, and you should schedule a meeting with the business owner or manager to discuss your needs and ask for their support.

d. You may want to tailor one type of brochure or letter to the businesses that have Christian ownership or employees that focuses more on spiritual matters of the school, and a slightly different letter or brochure to other businesses that focuses on academic achievements and the character of your students and graduates in society.

e. Be mindful that the business world is *scratch my back, I will scratch yours*, so think of doing something for them in return. Maybe a donor sign or board at your school on which their name is listed. Maybe place a plaque in their office or store saying they are a supporter of your Christian School. Maybe take out an ad in your local newspaper to thank those that have given to your school. These suggestions need to be discussed and approved (or not), and to what level, because many Christian schools may choose to refrain from the *commercialization* of their school, which may include disallowing advertisements. Your decision should be consistent, and be made known.

f. Many businesses could hire alumni from your school in the future. Tell them that supporting your school would be supporting the values and morals they admire in employees, and they could possibly hire students from your school in the future.

3) Individuals.
    a. Select specific people to send a personalized letter or brochure. After you describe your school and its benefits, describe some needs and ask to meet with that person to discuss those needs and how they can be involved.
    b. These people can be:
        i. Known Christian individuals.
        ii. Unknown Christian individuals.
        iii. Alumni of your school.
        iv. Relatives or friends of alumni, parents, staff, or students.
        v. Well-known figures or philanthropists in your area,
        vi. Church acquaintances.
        vii. People local churches could suggest to you.
    c. Suggestions for involvement in your school from these specific people can be:
        i. Prayer warrior.
        ii. Donation or other financial support. (Be sure to get them a receipt.)
        iii. Attempt to gain support from people they know.
        iv. Write a recommendation for your school for use in advertisements, promotional materials, etc.
        v. Help the school in any way they can through volunteerism, or other ways.
4) Estate, trust fund, will, and insurance donations.
    a. Many folks do not know they can designate at least a portion of their estate, trust fund, or life insurance to your Christian school.
    b. Meet with an Attorney specializing in these areas to understand the legality, and the "how to's" of doing

this with people. This is an area most people would love to do, they just don't know how, nor understand the legalities of it. With a little effort, you can become an expert at it.

c. Develop a brochure targeting this area of funding that describes your school's needs, and how to designate a portion of their estate to be given to your school. Possibly develop a handout describing the steps to designate, or will, a portion to your school.

5) Letter to parents and friends of your school
    a. I know most schools ask a lot from their parents, but you still need to present them with the needs of the school. This can be a letter at certain times of the year, or a paragraph in your schools weekly communication or web site such as a *Need of the Week*. Be sure to ask them to pray that you run your school as God wants you to as wise stewards, and the needs of your school be met. Then give them some ideas of other ways to help, which can be specific needs, underfunded areas, or future cut backs that they may want to help prevent from being cut. Consider sharing with them your budget and actual income to date. Many churches do this, but you will have to decide if it is appropriate. Remember, if you don't ask, you won't receive, so without sounding desperate in your letter, you can also:
        i. Ask them to contact anyone they know in a position to help out your school.
        ii. Ask them to have parents or grandparents list your school as a beneficiary to some extent.
        iii. Ask them to consider adding your school to the ministries they support.
        iv. Again, if you don't ask, you probably won't receive.

b. Monthly pledges as a result of a *Pledge Drive* or similar endeavor are a good way to receive donations of a fixed amount from individuals, as well as businesses. Set up automatic withdrawals with your bank, to make it easier for donors to give monthly and not forget. Be sure to discuss this with your bank, and possibly draft a *Letter of Pledge Commitment* that the donor signs. I would suggest an annual statement of giving be sent at the end of each year. If the pledge is for a specified period of time, be sure to outline that, and the remaining time and terms.

Other Possibilities:

6) Contact Christian Colleges or Universities
    a. Ask them if they offer scholarships specifically to Christian grade school students, possibly under the auspice that they commit to attending their college or university, and ask for their criteria.
    b. Ask if they support Christian grade schools financially, and what are their criteria.
7) Update and keep current your schools website.
    a. Have a *need* page where you can list some of the needs of the school and make it easy for folks to contact your school if they wish to donate. Make it possible for donations using their credit card and/or some on-line payment service such as PayPal. A story about your schools need, goal, building project, or mission's trip should always end with the opportunity for the reader to donate right then and there.
    b. Have a links page where a visitor can link to the web pages of companies that financially support your school. As mentioned earlier, this should be based

on the decisions of your schools governance as to recognition and/or advertising.

c. In this age of the internet, your schools web site is vitally important. It is your link to folks outside of your school, as well as parents or relatives of your students. It is an extremely important media of communication. Make full use of it. Assign or engage an individual to build and frequently maintain your schools web site, possibly as a donation, in which you send them a receipt for the value of their time. Lack of current information is the biggest complaint of web sites.

d. Have a blog on your web site. Blog authors could be staff, Trustees, parents, or even students. Designate one person to review and approve each blog post, possibly in line with established criteria and governing guidelines. Have a frequent blog post centered on the needs of the school and financial support.

8) Research for, and apply for grants, matching funds, and general donations. There is an incredible amount of money available in the form of grants, or similar funds. I have heard of Christian schools getting grants or donations for large wall pull-down maps, library grants, computer hardware and software grants or donations, multi-media donations (televisions and video players, movies or documentaries), athletic score boards, sports equipment, photo copiers, lunch food or reimbursement of lunch programs, or cafeteria equipment funding, grants for field trips including transportation expenses, and many more. Do not think that since you are a Christian school, there will be no state or federal funds for you. Contact your state and federal education authorities and inquire about grants. Contact the Christian school association you are affiliated with, and ask

them for advice and help on attaining grants or securing donations. Other ideas are:

a. There may be funds specifically for Christian schools. There may be funds for any schools and do not discriminate toward Christian schools.
b. Check with computer and software companies and ask them about donating their products to your school. Many firms donate (full, or partial cost) to get your students "hooked" on their product, which in most cases can be just fine, so do a little research on their product, and if you like what you find out, take advantage of that offer. Please remember to thank them.
c. Contact the manufacturer of products you use regularly in your school and ask them if they have a grant or donation program to schools. Most companies have a public relations department or person, so ask to speak to that person.
d. Research and seek out groups that offer grants. Some are corporations, book publishers, wholesalers, manufacturers' representatives, etc., and some are non-profit groups that exist to enhance learning or promotion of disciplines or topics. There are web sites devoted to grants for education, and sites that help you fill out applications for grants. There are grant consultants, so explore those services, and what they offer, and for what fee.
e. There are charity web sites where philanthropists, companies, and individuals can go to find places to donate to. Search out these, and get your school listed on them.
f. Designate a person (or ask for a volunteer) to tackle the endeavor of searching for, and applying for grants. It is time and effort well spent, but remember

discernment is important, so be diligent to read and inquire, and search for caveats or strings attached.

Be mindful of the donor's wishes concerning anonymity. Don't assume they want, or don't want recognition. It is alright to ask their wishes, and be sure to honor their request, as long as it is consistent with the decisions of your schools governance about recognition or advertisements. The donor may be considering Matthew 6:3 which indicates giving be done in secret so God gets the praise, not the giver.

Be diligent and timely concerning receipts for the donation, as well as a letter or card showing your heartfelt appreciation. Most donations can be tax deductible, so review the laws concerning them and issue a receipt appropriately, and timely. Keep accurate records of these donations and be able to refer to them in the event of an audit, or if the donor requests a receipt at a later date.

There are funds out there for your school. God is gracious, and wants an obedient and honoring Christian school to succeed if it glorifies Him. Using discernment, spend time going after those funds.

A sound Christian school is wise stewards of their finances. Embraces fundraising and donations as an opportunity for blessing for the donor and recipient, and a means of honoring and glorifying God.

Chapter 14

Elements of a Sound Christian School

The periodic table of elements is a listing of the components of our physical world. Each element is important, some to a larger degree than others, but all are essential as individual elements. Some combine with other elements to form something important to our world. Each element is part of Gods design for our physical world, and if an element is missing, there is imbalance, incompleteness, lack of structure, and possibly chaos.

Using the periodic table as a metaphor, the following list of *elements* is what makes up a Christian school. All are part of God's design for your Christian school. If any are missing, your school could be imbalanced, incomplete, unstructured, or chaotic.

Hopefully you didn't just jump to this chapter. I know it is tempting to look in the back of the book for the answers, but you wouldn't do that, right?! As suggestions, put each one of these qualities on a sticky note in various places around your office. Maybe put each one as a pop up reminder at various times in your computer or schedule. Another suggestion is a check off list, to be reviewed once a year, sort of an annual audit of the *soundness* of your Christian school.

The Word of God and God's principles are the standard of measurements used to evaluate and construct the character and distinguishing attributes of a sound Christian school.

We are to read the Bible, ponder it, and intellectually apply what we read to our daily life. To a Christian this is not optional, but required. It becomes the reasons and successes of Christian schools.

Sound Christian schools are *Christ Followers* and are rooted in the character and teachings of Jesus Christ as the foundation for all aspects of their schooling.

Sound Christian schools include the Bible for teaching, and for establishing God's laws, including what is right and wrong, in all classes and subjects, and believe it is sufficient for doing so.

Sound Christian schools don't allow students to continue in their selfish and sinful ways, but train them up in Gods ways.

Sound Christian schools don't make godly students, but lay the foundation of biblical truth from which the grace of God, the work of the Spirit, and the Gospel of Jesus Christ can make godly students.

Jesus is the Word of God, per the gospel of John chapter 1, and since morality (and our society's laws) must be rooted in the Word of God to function correctly, sound Christian schools teach that Jesus is the author of morality and society's laws.

Sound Christian education does not un-tether Jesus from the Word of God, laws, ethics, or morality. This becomes the basis for beliefs, growth in Christ, and for discernment.

Make sure your Christian school (or education) is the place to *plant* kids as God intends.

Each subject must be taught as if an extension of the Bible. Not an addition to the Bible, but an extension of the Bible.

The spiritual life (and sin in it) of teachers and students, is in a direct proportion to the amount of God's Word read and incorporated into the lessons taught.

Christian schools ensure the Bible is a systematically practiced reality, not just a concept.

Students in sound Christian education must have as their anchor or foundation or *distinguishing attribute*: Jesus, the Word of God.

Isaiah 33:6 says that wisdom and knowledge will be the stability of your times. The stability of your school is directly related to the biblical wisdom and biblical knowledge of your school's administration, teachers, and staff.

Sound Christian schools have true biblical Christians as administrators, teachers, and staff. The stability of the school depends on that requirement.

A sound Christian school will encompass and teach ALL elements of "the whole counsel of God", and will not denigrate, add to, or take way any part His Word.

A sound Christian school is built by biblical understanding, and furnished with biblical knowledge.

Sound Christian education teaches the 4 areas of life as Jesus learned in Luke 2:52: mental, physical, spiritual, and social.

When you commit your school to being biblically sound, Satan will attack, and try to get you and your school away from biblical soundness.

You can be strong and not waiver when you know God's Word, and continue to read and study it.

Sound Christian schools (including the leadership and staff) are strong in God's Word, and can recognize the "wiles of the devil", and are not susceptible easy targets for the Enemy.

Sound Christian schools have developed a hatred for sin, and an intolerance of sin.

A sound Christian school will teach their students that there is Truth, and what that Truth is.

If science and the Bible disagree, then the science is wrong.

Sound Christian schools need to firmly believe and teach that there IS right and wrong, there IS a basis of morality, and it MUST come from God and His Word.

Sound Christian education must include Truth and reality to combat against lies and illusion.

Sound Christian schools rightly divide Truth from error, and are not ashamed of standing firm on biblical Truth.

A sound Christian School has a keen sense of discernment able to accurately distinguish between Truth and error, and can spot the errors brought forth by Satan, and not teach them as fact or truth, or even as the best theory. (Matthew 18:6)

The greatest hope for the church, for evangelism, for our country, and for humanity, is in the proper solid biblically based teaching and raising of children, who when mature, can unwaveringly act like Jesus to expound the saving gospel of Jesus "in due season".

A sound Christian school will write God's laws on their students' hearts, minds, and consciences.

Sound Christian schools, (including the leadership and staff) are strong in God's Word, and can recognize the "wiles of the devil".

A true Christian school is a battlefield, not easy street.

A sound Christian school does not neglect teaching Satan is a real enemy and on the prowl like a roaring lion wanting to destroy those who love Jesus, but there is great hope found in the unmatched power and grace of Jesus.

Sound Christian schools need to recognize these schemes of the devil, and prepare students to defend against them.

Keep it simple, and keep it Biblical.

A sound Christian school teaches the use of the Whole Armor of God to stand against the attacks of the Enemy.

A sound Christian school prays for God's gracious hand of protection and safety of their school, but also wisely prepares for tragedy.

Healthy Sound Christian schools teach a diet of Biblical Truth as the foundation of proper thought, wisdom, attitudes, and actions.

The hand off of your subject to your students needs to come from a solid biblical foundation.

Sound Doctrine will build your students up, and give them strength and a solid foundation to stand on when treacherous times and people come.

A sound Christian school will have teachers that are endeavoring to be sound in faith, and try to teach as Jesus would have taught.

A sound Christian school will obey the commands of the Bible to love, and be characterized by the applicable elements of love from 1 Corinthians 13.

A sound Christian school will instill God's love and value in their students, even during discipline.

Sound Christian schools need to teach their students to be fully accountable and responsible for their actions, and are prepared to teach that to parents if required.

A sound Christian school will recognize the biblical requirement of endurance, learn it, and work at gaining it. Then, will also find a way to teach it to their students.

The teaching at your Christian school should show integrity, honesty, incorruptibility, soundness, righteousness, and completeness.

The speech of teachers in a sound Christian school should silence those that oppose Christianity and the Bible, and to make the gospel of Christ believable.

A sound Christian school <u>trains for life</u>, as well as for "the next test."

A sound Christian school will be one of the options parents have for their kids as they endeavor to be obedient to God in the training and discipline of the LORD. Make sure your school is the proper place for them to *plant* their kids as God intends.

"Quality goes in before the name goes on."

A sound Christian school has as a priority the training of the students' HEART, and understands that *heart work is hard work*, and is diligent to that endeavor.

Sound Christian schools employ teachers that enthusiastically gain and use the tools required to teach effectively.

Sound Christian school teachers endeavor to give 100% effort to attain biblically accurate Truth, and to relate that Truth effectively to their students in all scholastic subjects.

A sound Christian school's Administrator and staff upholds Gods perfect plan of marriage and family structure.

A sound Christian school goes along side parents in training their children to impact the world for Jesus. Obedience and discipline are equally important in the home and at school.

The school Administrator is to love, serve, and to ensure his or her staff and teachers flourish.

A sound Christian school follows God's requirements for their Administrator or leadership, and keeps them accountable to those requirements, even if dismissal and a replacement is necessary.

A sound Christian school will be unified, and honor each other as they honor the Lord.

A sound Christian school will be lights unto the world, being involved in their community first, and then the world.

A sound Christian school will endeavor to have the mind of Christ, and teach that to their students.

A sound Christian school has spent the time to develop, refine, and publicly declare the core doctrines, beliefs, and values that define their school.

A sound Christian school is known more for what they are FOR, than what they are against.

A sound Christian school will have staff and leaders that are unified around Jesus Christ and the Word of God. Their unity will be evident, even to those not affiliated with the school.

Sound Christian schools will ensure well rounded training of growth in these four areas: *mental, physical, spiritual, and social.*

A sound Christian school has specific vision, and the plans and means to accomplish that vision, through the Lord and His Word.

A sound Christian school will graduate students that are confident, strong, courageous, and godly people that will make an impact, and will take a stand for God when needed. A person, as Jesus said in Matthew 5, whose yes is yes, and no is no.

A sound Christian school has a policy manual or handbook outlining the requirements and rules of the school. Where applicable, the items in the handbook are biblically based, and explained.

A sound Christian school will inform children *why* something is taught to them, *what* the consequences are if they do not follow it, and *how* to think through and make correct related decisions. A sound Christian school uses these three, and does so during both pre-emptive teaching to students, and when disciplining students.

Sound Christian schools explain the *reasons* for their rules.

Rules of conduct, why those rules exist, explanation and understanding when rules are broken, humble repentance of specific wrongdoing, properly explaining why and administering discipline, reconciliation with love, accountability to ensure non-repeating the wrongdoing, praise when correction and proper attitude is recognized, and the resultant character building is a biblical process that is part of a sound Christian school.

Sound Christian schools have a policy on discipline, because it is an integral component of learning, of self-control, of a moral compass, of character building, and of training the heart.

Sound Christian schools train students to think for themselves, and to make correct decisions for themselves.

The closer a sound Christian school is to God, the more of His character attributes the school has, and the more visible they are to others.

A sound Christian school has a policy on character building which includes the processes of handling a stimulating situation, instilling confidence, and creating a feeling of personal value.

Sound Christian schools train students how to be discerning, to think things through, and use proper judgment, viewing everything through the "spectacles" of Scripture.

Tie God's Word to rules of conduct. Since God is the author of foundational rules, He must be included in those of your school, or you will not get the results intended.

Sound Christian schools teach the biblical process of handling situations of life, which begins with thinking controlling emotions.

Sound Christian schools teach that actions have consequences, including sinful actions. Christian staff recognizes sin in their students, and tactfully addresses the sin, and explains the consequences of it, as well as God's righteous judgment of sin.

Discipline is an integral component of learning, of self-control, of a moral compass, of character building, of training the heart, and therefore an element of a sound Christian school.

A sound Christian school teaches their students to have correct and biblical character.

It is *always* right to do right, it is *never* right to do wrong, and *never* wrong to do right.

Teach students to obey God's Word no matter what, no matter when, no matter where, and no matter who.

Sound Christian schools teach children to obey and honor their parents. This is the main command given to children in the Bible, and so it should be paramount in your school.

Repentance should be a goal of every disciplinary situation. God requires it, and we should too. This teaches them the valuable thought process, and teaches them to develop their moral compass. Repentance is required for resolution, forgiveness, closure, learning, and advancement.

A teacher in a sound Christian school will use the Bible in every subject and activity.

Teachers, the "hand off" of your subject to your students needs to come from a solid biblical footing.

Teaching a student that they are valuable is a must. Every person wants to have value, and Christian schooling should ensure that each and every student has value, especially during the teen years when they are struggling to understand their value, and look for it in various places: so be one of the places that they feel secure and valuable.

Students attending and graduated from a sound Christian school will be adorned with the doctrine of God.

Character is patterned after God's Word, and our character grows more pleasing to Him when the more like Jesus we become.

A sound Christian school is wise stewards of their finances. Embracing fundraising and donations as an opportunity for blessings for the donor and recipient, and a means of honoring and glorifying God.

God is gracious, and wants an obedient and honoring Christian school to succeed if it glorifies Him.

A sound Christian school teaches their students to make godly choices on their own.

Have you seen those amusement park photo opportunity areas where there is a full size photo or painting of something like a clown, or a muscular weight lifter, or a famous person, and you go around behind and put your face through so that character has your face? Those are a lot of fun to see what you would look like with the body of that character. Sometimes it is so out of place that you can't help but laugh at the absurdity.

Now, with that in your mind, picture one of those photo opportunity boards with several holes for faces, and the previous list of elements of a sound Christian school written all over the board. Now picture students of your graduation class putting their faces through that board, and ask yourself "is it agreeable with them, or is it absurdity?" It will be agreeable if your school has the **Qualities of Sound Christian Education.**

Additional Recommended Resources

- Foundational Issues in Christian Education – Robert W. Pazmino
- Kingdom Education – Glen Schultz
- Repairing the Ruins – Douglas Wilson
- Recovering the Lost Tools of Learning: An Approach to Distinctively Christian Education – Douglas Wilson
- Making the Connections: How to Put Biblical Worldview Integration into Practice – Don Johnson & Christian Overman
- Punished by Rewards: The Trouble with Gold Stars, Incentive Plan's, A's, Praise and Other Bribes – Alfie Kohn (This is not from a Christian perspective but poses intriguing questions and calls for questioning our thinking)
- Philosophy & Education: an introduction in Christian Perspective – George R. Knight
- Orations on Philosophy and Education – Philip Melanchton (Melanchton was a contemporary of Martin Luther)
- A Theology for Christian Education – James R. Estep Jr., Michael J. Anthony and Greg R. Allison

About the Author

Kevin Brownlee has a passion for Christian education. Coming from a family of educators and school administrators, and a graduate from a Christian university, he has served as a Christian school Trustee. He has done extensive research on what is required to start, run, and maintain a Christian school that is founded on sound biblical doctrine (and what that doctrine is). Serving as a School Trustee at Heritage Christian School in Bozeman, Montana he paired his research with what God taught him from God's Word on education and added the extensive hands-on experiences of overseeing that Christian K-12 school. Kevin has compiled that knowledge and experience into a training seminar for Christian educators and school leaders, and this book "Qualities of Sound Christian Education".

Kevin became a Christian in 1964, has a Bachelor's degree from LeTourneau University, is a small business owner, and has been married for 27 years with one teenage Daughter. He has taught small group Bible studies for over 26 years, and has written several small group Bible study courses. He has given seminars, devotionals, and short sermons countless times over the years, is the owner and author of the blog "Sound Christian Schooling" at www.kevinbrownlee.com and still finds time to enjoy mountain biking, hiking, and skiing in God's beautiful creation of the mountains of Montana.

Endnotes

1 Random House Webster's College Dictionary. "Education." Definitions.net. STANDS4 LLC, 2013. Web. 26 Mar. 2013. <http://www.definitions.net/definition/Education>.

2 1828 edition of Webster's American Dictionary of the English Language, <http://1828.mshaffer.com/d/search/word,education>.

3 "HISTORY OF THE REFORMATION IN THE SIXTEENTH CENTURY," by J. H. Merle d'Aubigné, 1846. French edition 1835. Published by Baker Book House (USA), reprinted from the edition issued in London in 1846. p 190.

4 Holman Bible Dictionary: Education in Bible Times <http://www.studylight.org/dic/hbd/view.cgi?number=T1737

5 http://www2.whidbey.net/jmboyes/warn1.htm>.

6 Millstones & Stumbling Blocks: Understanding Education in Post-Christian America. Bradley Heath. Pg. 109. 2006 Fenestra Books, Tucson, Arizona 85705

7 http://www.merriam-webster.com/dictionary/

8 http://www.merriam-webster.com/dictionary/

9 http://www.gty.org/resources/positions/P10/you-can-trust-the-bible

10 The Bible: The Inerrant Word of God by J. Hampton Keathley, III < http://bible.org/seriespage/bible-inerrant-word-god>.

11 <http://headhearthand.posterous.com/short-joel-beeke-video-on-hell>.

12 The Macarthur study Bible, John MacArthur Author and General Editor, New King James Version, Copyright 1997 Word Publishing.

13 http://www.merriam-webster.com/dictionary/

14 Poll: September 28, 2010 < www.pewforum.org/other-beliefs-and-practices/u-s-religious-knowledge-survey.aspx>.

15 "Is God a Mathematician?" by Keith Newman.< www.wordworx.co.nz.panin.html> (Regarding Dr. Ivan Panin)

16 http://carlarolfe.com/swesley.pdf

17 http://www.merriam-webster.com/dictionary/

18 <www.thetruthproject.org>

19 <www.barna.org> "A Biblical Worldview Has a Radical Effect on a Person's Life," December 1, 2003.

20 http://www.merriam-webster.com/dictionary/

21 http://www.merriam-webster.com/dictionary/

22 http://www.merriam-webster.com/dictionary/

23 http://www.merriam-webster.com/dictionary/

24 http://www.merriam-webster.com/dictionary/

25 http://www.merriam-webster.com/dictionary/

26 Management: A Biblical Approach. Myron Rush. Pg. 12, Eighth printing 1988 Victor Books, a division of SP Publications, Inc. Wheaton, Illinois 60187

27 Management: A Biblical Approach. Myron Rush. Pg. 13, Eighth printing 1988 Victor Books, a division of SP Publications, Inc. Wheaton, Illinois 60187

28 Management: A Biblical Approach. Myron Rush. Pg. 13-15, Eighth printing 1988 Victor Books, a division of SP Publications, Inc. Wheaton, Illinois 60187

29 Addictions: a Banquet in the Grave. Finding Hope in the Power of the Gospel. Edward T. Welch, P. 155, P&R Publishing Company, Phillipsburg, New Jersey 08865